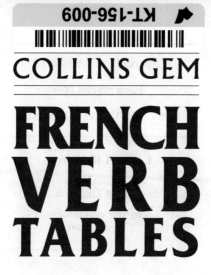

COLLINS GEM

FRENCH VERB TABLES

HarperCollins*Publishers*

first published in this edition 1994

© HarperCollins Publishers 1994

latest reprint 1996

ISBN 0 00 470993-4 Paperback

Lesley A Robertson

editorial staff
Megan Thomson

editorial management
Vivian Marr

Typeset by Tradespools Ltd, Frome, Somerset

*Printed and bound in Great Britain by
Caledonian International Book Manufacturing Ltd,
Glasgow, G64*

INTRODUCTION

The **Collins Gem French Verb Tables** is an essential reference book for all learners of French. It gives you all the information you need about French verbs and how to use them in a clear, user-friendly layout.

The main part of the book consists of 112 fully conjugated French verbs – regular and irregular – listed alphabetically. Each is self-contained in a double-page spread showing in full all the tenses with pronouns, so you can see at a glance which verb ending to use for which tense and which person. The spread also lists common constructions and idiomatic phrases containing that verb, plus other verbs which are conjugated in a similar way.

In addition, the introduction gives a detailed explanation of each of the three French verb conjugations, along with instructions on how to form the present participle, the past participle and the imperative in each conjugation. Defective verbs and 'regular' spelling irregularities are also listed.

The final section of the book comprises an alphabetical index of over 2,000 widely used verbs, each one cross-referred to its basic model.

CONTENTS

The French Verb	4
'Regular' Spelling Irregularities	8
Glossary	9
Compound Tenses: The Use of Auxiliary Verbs	10
Defective Verbs	13
VERB TABLES	14
Index	238

THE FRENCH VERB

The majority of verbs are regular and conform to rules; the fact that irregular verbs do not follow any overall pattern means that they have to be learned individually.

The infinitive ending of regular verbs indicates to which conjugation or group they belong:
1st conjugation: ER ending; model: DONNER (36)★
2nd conjugation: IR ending; model: FINIR (45)★
3rd conjugation: RE ending; model: VENDRE (107)★
(★ = verb model number, not page number)

To conjugate a regular verb, you must add the appropriate verb ending to the appropriate tense stem. The stem for the present, imperfect, past historic and both subjunctive tenses is the infinitive minus its ER, IR or RE ending; the stem for the future and conditional tenses is the whole infinitive in the 1st and 2nd conjugations, and the infinitive minus its final E in the 3rd conjugation.

For each conjugation, the following tables show
  (1) the verb endings for each tense
  (2) how these are added to the stem

Pr = present; I = imperfect; F = future; C = conditional; PH = past historic; PrS = present subjunctive; PS = past subjunctive

1st conjugation (1)

Tense	Endings					
Pr	e	es	e	ons	ez	ent
I	ais	ais	ait	ions	iez	aient
F	ai	as	a	ons	ez	ont
C	ais	ais	ait	ions	iez	aient
PH	ai	as	a	âmes	âtes	èrent
PrS	e	es	e	ions	iez	ent
PS	asse	asses	ât	assions	assiez	assent

(2)

	STEM	Pr	I	PH	Pr S	P S
je	donn	e	ais	ai	e	asse
tu	donn	es	ais	as	es	asses
il	donn	e	ait	a	e	ât
nous	donn	ons	ions	âmes	ions	assions
vous	donn	ez	iez	âtes	iez	assiez
ils	donn	ent	aient	èrent	ent	assent

	STEM	F	C
je	donner	ai	ais
tu	donner	as	ais
il	donner	a	ait
nous	donner	ons	ions
vous	donner	ez	iez
ils	donner	ont	aient

2nd conjugation (1)

Tense	Endings					
Pr	is	is	it	issons	issez	issent
I	issais	issais	issait	issions	issiez	issaient
F	ai	as	a	ons	ez	ont
C	ais	ais	ait	ions	iez	aient
PH	is	is	it	îmes	îtes	irent
PrS	isse	isses	isse	issions	issiez	issent
PS	isse	isses	it	issions	issiez	issent

(2)

	STEM	Pr	I	PH	Pr S	P S
je	fin	is	issais	is	isse	isse
tu	fin	is	issais	is	isses	isses
il	fin	it	issait	it	isse	ît
nous	fin	issons	issions	îmes	issions	issions
vous	fin	issez	issiez	îtes	issiez	issiez
ils	fin	issent	issaient	irent	issent	issent

	STEM	F	C
je	**finir**	ai	ais
tu	**finir**	as	ais
il	**finir**	a	ait
nous	**finir**	ons	ions
vous	**finir**	ez	iez
ils	**finir**	ont	aient

3rd conjugation (1)

Tense	Endings					
Pr	s	s	—	ons	ez	ent
I	ais	ais	ait	ions	iez	aient
F	ai	as	a	ons	ez	ont
C	ais	ais	ait	ions	iez	aient
PH	is	is	it	îmes	îtes	irent
PrS	e	es	e	ions	iez	ent
PS	isse	isses	it	issions	issiez	issent

(2)

	STEM	Pr	I	PH	Pr S	P S
je	**vend**	s	ais	is	e	isse
tu	**vend**	s	ais	is	es	isses
il	**vend**		ait	it	e	ît
nous	**vend**	ons	ions	îmes	ions	issions
vous	**vend**	ez	iez	îtes	iez	issiez
ils	**vend**	ent	aient	irent	ent	issent

	STEM	F	C
je	**vendr**	ai	ais
tu	**vendr**	as	ais
il	**vendr**	a	ait
nous	**vendr**	ons	ions
vous	**vendr**	ez	iez
ils	**vendr**	ont	aient

THE PRESENT PARTICIPLE

To form the present participle, add the following endings to the infinitive minus its ER, IR or RE ending

    1st conjugation **ant**   (donnant)
    2nd conjugation **issant** (finissant)
    3rd conjugation **ant**   (vendant)

With the exception of 'en', French uses an infinitive after prepositions where English uses a present participle.

Thus: sans parler = without speaking
        après être parti = after having left

but: en faisant = while doing.

THE PAST PARTICIPLE

To form the past participle, add the following endings to the infinitive minus its ER, IR or RE ending

    1st conjugation **é** (donné)
    2nd conjugation **i** (fini)
    3rd conjugation **u** (vendu)

For agreement rules in compound tenses, see p. 10.

THE IMPERATIVE

The imperative is the same as the present tense 'tu', 'nous' and 'vous' forms minus the subject pronouns: finis, allons, commencez.

Exceptions
1) ER verbs and verbs like cueillir, ouvrir etc, which keep the 's' ending of the 'tu' form only if it is immediately followed by y or en: avance, va; vas-y, cueilles-en.
2) avoir and être, whose imperative forms are the same as the present subjunctive (minus the 's' of 'tu' form for avoir).
3) vouloir: veuille, veuillons, veuillez.
4) savoir: sache, sachons, sachez.

Affirmative/negative imperative – pronoun object follows/precedes verb: prends-le/ne le prends pas; asseyez-vous/ne vous asseyez pas.

'REGULAR' SPELLING IRREGULARITIES

A number of spelling changes affect 1st conjugation verbs. Such changes and when they occur are shown below. Verb types are divided according to their infinitive ending. We suggest that you use the table in conjunction with the numbered verb models indicated. C = consonant(s).

-eler/-eter *(i: appeler 4/jeter 50;* *ii: acheter 1)* *either* i) l→ll/t→tt *or* ii) e→è	*before* e, es, ent; *throughout future and* *conditional tenses*
e + C + er *(lever 52)* e→è	*as above*
-éger *(protéger 80)* é→è; *see* **-ger**	*before* e, es, ent; *as for* **-ger**
-é + C + er *(espérer 41)* é→è	*before* e, es, ent
-oyer/-uyer *(nettoyer 63)* y→i	*before* e, es, ent; *throughout future and* *conditional tenses*
-ayer *(i: payer 70; ii: as for nettoyer* *63)* *either* i) y retained throughout *or* ii) y→i	*as above*
-cer *(commencer 15)* c→ç *(to soften c)*	*when verb endings* *starting with a or o* *immediately follow c*
-ger *(manger 54)* e retained *(to soften g)*	*when verb endings* *starting with a or o* *immediately follow g*

GLOSSARY

You should familiarize yourself with the following descriptions of major verb categories.

Transitive taking a direct object

Intransitive used without a direct object

* A verb may be transitive in English yet intransitive in French (and vice versa):
he disobeyed the rules (transitive)
il a désobéi aux règles (intransitive)
he looked at his sister (intransitive)
il a regardé sa sœur (transitive)

Reflexive taking a reflexive pronoun (English: myself, ourselves etc; French: me, nous etc) which 'reflects' back to the subject

* 1) Not all verbs which are reflexive in French are reflexive in English
e.g. se coucher = to go to bed
   2) The reflexive pronoun is sometimes optional in English
e.g. se laver = to wash (oneself)

Reciprocal taking a reciprocal pronoun which expresses mutual action or relation
e.g. ils se regardent = they look at each other *or* one another

* Since the plural forms of reciprocal and reflexive verbs are identical, 'ils se regardent' might mean 'they look at themselves'. Always gauge the correct translation from the context.

Auxiliary used to conjugate verbs in their compound tenses (see p. 10)

Impersonal used only in the 3rd person singular, to represent a neutral subject
e.g. il pleut = it's raining

COMPOUND TENSES: THE USE OF AUXILIARY VERBS

In simple tenses, the verb is expressed in one word (e.g. donne, finira, vendions); in compound tenses, the past participle is added to the appropriate tense of the auxiliary verbs avoir and être (e.g. a donné, aura fini, avions vendu). Most verbs are conjugated with avoir, but the être auxiliary is used with reflexive and reciprocal verbs, and when the verb is in the passive voice. (See note on Passive: p. 12)

The following intransitive verbs are also conjugated with être:

aller	revenir	passer★
venir	retourner★	rester
entrer★	rentrer★	devenir
sortir★	monter★	naître
arriver	descendre★	mourir
partir	tomber	

(★ = conjugated with avoir when transitive)

RULES OF AGREEMENT FOR PAST PARTICIPLES

(a) The past participle of a verb conjugated with être agrees in number and gender with its subject.

Thus: elle est partie = she left
elle s'est souvenue[1] = she remembered
([1]typical of verbs which are reflexive in form but whose pronouns have no true reflexive value)

Exceptions: 1) reflexives   2) reciprocals
  e.g. 1) elle s'est lavée (transitive)
       elle s'est parlé (intransitive)
  2) ils se sont regardés (transitive)
     ils se sont parlé (intransitive)
  (Exceptions explained in (b))

(b) The past participle of a verb conjugated with avoir and of a transitive reflexive or reciprocal verb agrees in number and gender with its direct object, provided the direct object

10

precedes the verb; otherwise, the past participle remains invariable.

Thus: je les ai vendus = I sold them
    elle s'est lavée = she washed
    ils se sont regardés = they looked at each other

but: j'ai vendu les sacs = I sold the bags
    elle s'est parlé = she talked to herself
    (s' = indirect object)
    ils se sont parlé = they talked to each other
    (se = indirect object)
    (*NB*: elle s'est lavé les mains = she washed her hands – no agreement since direct object (les mains) follows the verb and s' = indirect object)

Some intransitive verbs (e.g. coûter, peser etc) may be accompanied by a complement of price, weight etc. Do not mistake this for a direct object: the past participle remains invariable – 'les 5 F que ça m'a coûté = the 5 F it cost me'; 'les 3 kilos que le colis a pesé = the 3 kilos the parcel weighed'. Also invariable are the past participles of impersonal verbs – 'les accidents qu'il y a eu = the accidents there were'.

For verbal constructions of the type 'I saw her leave', 'she heard them being scolded' (verbs of perception), or 'he took us swimming', which are translated in French by a verb plus infinitive, the rules of agreement are as follows:

1) if the preceding direct object is the subject of the infinitive, the past participle agrees in number and gender with it:
    je l'ai vue partir = I saw her leave
    il nous a emmenés nager = he took us swimming

2) if the preceding direct object is the object of the infinitive, the past participle remains invariable:
    elle les a entendu gronder
    = she heard them being scolded.

In constructions such as 'laisser faire' where laisser is used in conjunction with an infinitive, the same rules apply:

1) je les ai laissés tomber = I dropped them
2) elle s'est laissé persuader = she let herself be persuaded.

When faire is used in this way, however, it contradicts the 1st rule: the past participle remains invariable in both cases:
1) la femme qu'il a fait venir = the women he sent for
2) la montre qu'il a fait réparer = the watch he (has) had repaired.

THE PASSIVE VOICE

A transitive verb is active when its subject performs the action (she disobeyed the rules) and passive when its subject receives the action (she was punished). In French, the passive is formed by adding the past participle to the appropriate tense of être: 'elle était punie = she was punished' (note agreement with subject).

(*NB*: do not confuse a passive verb with an intransitive verb, which can only be used in the active voice –
elle était allée = she had gone)

French does not use the passive as extensively as English, preferring

either 1) 'on': on m'a dit que … = I was told that …

or 2) a reflexive verb with an inanimate subject:
ce mot ne s'emploie plus = this word is no longer used.

Note

In the tables on the following pages these abbreviations are used.

qch	quelque chose
qn	quelqu'un
sb	somebody
sth	something

DEFECTIVE VERBS

Defective verbs have missing or obsolete parts. The forms shown below are those most likely to occur. Unless otherwise stated, the auxiliary verb (where applicable) is avoir.

1 Present Participle *2* Past Participle *3* Present *4* Imperfect *5* Future *6* Conditional *7* Past Historic *8* Present Subjunctive *9* Past Subjunctive

accroire en faire accroire
apparoir *3* il appert
béer *1* béant *3* il bée *4* il béait
choir (être) *2* chu *3* chois, chois, choit, choient *5* choirai *etc* *6* choirais *etc* *7* il chut *9* chût
déchoir *2* déchu *3* déchois, déchois, déchoit, déchoyons, déchoyez, déchoient *5* déchoirai *etc* *6* déchoirais *etc* *7* déchus *etc* *8* déchoie *etc* *9* déchusse *etc*
échoir (être) *1* échéant *2* échu *3* il échoit *5* il échoira *6* il échoirait *7* il échut *8* il échoie *9* il échût
faillir *1* faillant *2* failli *5* faillirai *etc* *6* faillirais *etc* *7* faillis *etc* NB: j'ai failli tomber = I nearly fell
gésir *1* gisant *3* gis, gis, gît, gisons, gisez *4* gisais *etc*
messeoir *1* messéant *3* il messied, ils messiéent *6* il messiérait, ils messiéraient
oindre *1* oignant *2* oint *3* il oint *4* il oignait
ouïr *2* ouï
paître *1* paissant *3* pais, pais, paît, paissons, paissez, paissent *4* paissais *etc* *5* paîtrai *etc* *6* paîtrais *etc* *8* paisse *etc*
poindre *2* point *3* il point *5* il poindra
repaître *like* paître *but also has 2* repu *7* repus *etc* *9* repusse *etc*
seoir (= *to become*) *1* seyant *3* il sied, ils siéent *4* il seyait, ils seyaient *5* il siéra, ils siéront *6* il siérait, ils siéraient *8* il siée

13

1 acheter
to buy

also **congeler**
to freeze

PRESENT PARTICIPLE
achetant

déceler
to discover

PAST PARTICIPLE
acheté

geler
to freeze

PRESENT		IMPERFECT	
j'	achète	j'	achetais
tu	achètes	tu	achetais
il	achète	il	achetait
nous	achetons	nous	achetions
vous	achetez	vous	achetiez
ils	achètent	ils	achetaient

		FUTURE	
		j'	achèterai
		tu	achèteras
		il	achètera
		nous	achèterons
		vous	achèterez
		ils	achèteront

IMPERATIVE		CONDITIONAL	
	achète	j'	achèterais
	achetons	tu	achèterais
	achetez	il	achèterait
		nous	achèterions
		vous	achèteriez
		ils	achèteraient

haleter
to paint

peler
to peel

PAST HISTORIC		PRESENT SUBJUNCTIVE	
j'	achetai	j'	achète
tu	achetas	tu	achètes
il	acheta	il	achète
nous	achetâmes	nous	achetions
vous	achetâtes	vous	achetiez
ils	achetèrent	ils	achètent

PERFECT		PAST SUBJUNCTIVE	
j'	ai acheté	j'	achetasse
tu	as acheté	tu	achetasses
il	a acheté	il	achetât
nous	avons acheté	nous	achetassions
vous	avez acheté	vous	achetassiez
ils	ont acheté	ils	achetassent

CONSTRUCTIONS

acheter qch à qn to buy sth from sb; to buy sth for sb
je le lui ai acheté I bought it from him; I bought it for him
je le lui ai acheté 10 F I bought it from him for 10 F

2 acquérir
to acquire

also **conquérir**
to conquer

PRESENT PARTICIPLE
acquérant

s'enquérir
to inquire

PAST PARTICIPLE
acquis

requérir
to require

PRESENT		IMPERFECT	
j'	acquiers	j'	acquérais
tu	acquiers	tu	acquérais
il	acquiert	il	acquérait
nous	acquérons	nous	acquérions
vous	acquérez	vous	acquériez
ils	acquièrent	ils	acquéraient

		FUTURE	
		j'	acquerrai
		tu	acquerras
		il	acquerra
		nous	acquerrons
		vous	acquerrez
		ils	acquerront

IMPERATIVE	CONDITIONAL	
acquiers	j'	acquerrais
acquérons	tu	acquerrais
acquérez	il	acquerrait
	nous	acquerrions
	vous	acquerriez
	ils	acquerraient

PAST HISTORIC		PRESENT SUBJUNCTIVE	
j'	acquis	j'	acquière
tu	acquis	tu	acquières
il	acquit	il	acquière
nous	acquîmes	nous	acquérions
vous	acquîtes	vous	acquériez
ils	acquirent	ils	acquièrent

PERFECT		PAST SUBJUNCTIVE	
j'	ai acquis	j'	acquisse
tu	as acquis	tu	acquisses
il	a acquis	il	acquît
nous	avons acquis	nous	acquissions
vous	avez acquis	vous	acquissiez
ils	ont acquis	ils	acquissent

CONSTRUCTIONS

acquérir de l'expérience to gain experience
acquérir de la valeur to go up in value
les mauvaises habitudes s'acquièrent facilement bad habits are easily picked up

3 aller
to go

PRESENT PARTICIPLE
allant

PAST PARTICIPLE
allé

PRESENT		*IMPERFECT*	
je	**vais**	j'	**allais**
tu	**vas**	tu	**allais**
il	**va**	il	**allait**
nous	**allons**	nous	**allions**
vous	**allez**	vous	**alliez**
ils	**vont**	ils	**allaient**

		FUTURE	
		j'	**irai**
		tu	**iras**
		il	**ira**
		nous	**irons**
		vous	**irez**
		ils	**iront**

IMPERATIVE		*CONDITIONAL*	
	va	j'	**irais**
	allons	tu	**irais**
	allez	il	**irait**
		nous	**irions**
		vous	**iriez**
		ils	**iraient**

aller 3
to go

PAST HISTORIC	*PRESENT SUBJUNCTIVE*
j' **allai**	j' **aille**
tu **allas**	tu **ailles**
il **alla**	il **aille**
nous **allâmes**	nous **allions**
vous **allâtes**	vous **alliez**
ils **allèrent**	ils **aillent**
PERFECT	*PAST SUBJUNCTIVE*
je **suis allé**	j' **allasse**
tu **es allé**	tu **allasses**
il **est allé**	il **allât**
nous **sommes allés**	nous **allassions**
vous **êtes allé(s)**	vous **allassiez**
ils **sont allés**	ils **allassent**

CONSTRUCTIONS
aller faire qch to go and do sth
aller à qn to fit sb; to suit sb
comment allez-vous? – je vais bien/mal/mieux how are you? – I'm well/unwell/better
s'en aller to go (away); to leave
allons-y! let's go!

4 appeler
to call

also **amonceler**
to pile up

PRESENT PARTICIPLE
appelant

épeler
to spell

PAST PARTICIPLE
appelé

jumeler
to twin

PRESENT		IMPERFECT	
j'	appelle	j'	appelais
tu	appelles	tu	appelais
il	appelle	il	appelait
nous	appelons	nous	appelions
vous	appelez	vous	appeliez
ils	appellent	ils	appelaient

FUTURE	
j'	appellerai
tu	appelleras
il	appellera
nous	appellerons
vous	appellerez
ils	appelleront

IMPERATIVE	CONDITIONAL	
appelle	j'	appellerais
appelons	tu	appellerais
appelez	il	appellerait
	nous	appellerions
	vous	appelleriez
	ils	appelleraient

rappeler
to recall

renouveler
to renew

PAST HISTORIC		PRESENT SUBJUNCTIVE	
j'	appelai	j'	appelle
tu	appelas	tu	appelles
il	appela	il	appelle
nous	appelâmes	nous	appelions
vous	appelâtes	vous	appeliez
ils	appelèrent	ils	appellent

PERFECT		PAST SUBJUNCTIVE	
j'	ai appelé	j'	appelasse
tu	as appelé	tu	appelasses
il	a appelé	il	appelât
nous	avons appelé	nous	appelassions
vous	avez appelé	vous	appelassiez
ils	ont appelé	ils	appelassent

CONSTRUCTIONS

comment vous appelez-vous?   what's your name?
je m'appelle Suzanne   my name is Suzanne
appeler qn à l'aide *or* **au secours**   to call to sb for help
en appeler à   to appeal to

5 apprendre

to learn

PRESENT PARTICIPLE
apprenant

PAST PARTICIPLE
appris

PRESENT		IMPERFECT	
j'	apprends	j'	apprenais
tu	apprends	tu	apprenais
il	apprend	il	apprenait
nous	apprenons	nous	apprenions
vous	apprenez	vous	appreniez
ils	apprennent	ils	apprenaient

		FUTURE	
		j'	apprendrai
		tu	apprendras
		il	apprendra
		nous	apprendrons
		vous	apprendrez
		ils	apprendront

IMPERATIVE	CONDITIONAL	
apprends	j'	apprendrais
apprenons	tu	apprendrais
apprenez	il	apprendrait
	nous	apprendrions
	vous	apprendriez
	ils	apprendraient

PAST HISTORIC		PRESENT SUBJUNCTIVE	
j'	appris	j'	apprenne
tu	appris	tu	apprennes
il	apprit	il	apprenne
nous	apprîmes	nous	apprenions
vous	apprîtes	vous	appreniez
ils	apprirent	ils	apprennent

PERFECT		PAST SUBJUNCTIVE	
j'	ai appris	j'	apprisse
tu	as appris	tu	apprisses
il	a appris	il	apprît
nous	avons appris	nous	apprissions
vous	avez appris	vous	apprissiez
ils	ont appris	ils	apprissent

CONSTRUCTIONS

apprendre à faire qch   to learn (how) to do sth
apprendre qch à qn   to teach sb sth; to tell sb sth
apprendre à qn à faire qch   to teach sb (how) to do sth
l'espagnol s'apprend facilement   Spanish is easy to learn

6 arriver

to arrive

PRESENT PARTICIPLE
arrivant

PAST PARTICIPLE
arrivé

	PRESENT		*IMPERFECT*
j'	arrive	j'	arrivais
tu	arrives	tu	arrivais
il	arrive	il	arrivait
nous	arrivons	nous	arrivions
vous	arrivez	vous	arriviez
ils	arrivent	ils	arrivaient

	FUTURE
j'	arriverai
tu	arriveras
il	arrivera
nous	arriverons
vous	arriverez
ils	arriveront

	IMPERATIVE		*CONDITIONAL*
	arrive	j'	arriverais
	arrivons	tu	arriverais
	arrivez	il	arriverait
		nous	arriverions
		vous	arriveriez
		ils	arriveraient

PAST HISTORIC		PRESENT SUBJUNCTIVE	
j'	arrivai	j'	arrive
tu	arrivas	tu	arrives
il	arriva	il	arrive
nous	arrivâmes	nous	arrivions
vous	arrivâtes	vous	arriviez
ils	arrivèrent	ils	arrivent

PERFECT		PAST SUBJUNCTIVE	
je	suis arrivé	j'	arrivasse
tu	es arrivé	tu	arrivasses
il	est arrivé	il	arrivât
nous	sommes arrivés	nous	arrivassions
vous	êtes arrivé(s)	vous	arrivassiez
ils	sont arrivés	ils	arrivassent

CONSTRUCTIONS

arriver à faire qch   to succeed in doing sth
ça peut arriver   this may happen
il lui est arrivé un accident   he's had an accident
la neige lui arrivait (jusqu')aux genoux   the snow came
up to his knees

25

7 assaillir

to attack

PRESENT PARTICIPLE
assaillant

PAST PARTICIPLE
assailli

PRESENT		IMPERFECT	
j'	assaille	j'	assaillais
tu	assailles	tu	assaillais
il	assaille	il	assaillait
nous	assaillons	nous	assaillions
vous	assaillez	vous	assailliez
ils	assaillent	ils	assaillaient

		FUTURE	
		j'	assaillirai
		tu	assailliras
		il	assaillira
		nous	assaillirons
		vous	assaillirez
		ils	assailliront

IMPERATIVE		CONDITIONAL	
	assaille	j'	assaillirais
	assaillons	tu	assaillirais
	assaillez	il	assaillirait
		nous	assaillirions
		vous	assailliriez
		ils	assailliraient

PAST HISTORIC		PRESENT SUBJUNCTIVE	
j'	assaillis	j'	assaille
tu	assaillis	tu	assailles
il	assaillit	il	assaille
nous	assaillîmes	nous	assaillions
vous	assaillîtes	vous	assailliez
ils	assaillirent	ils	assaillent

PERFECT		PAST SUBJUNCTIVE	
j'	ai assailli	j'	assaillisse
tu	as assailli	tu	assaillisses
il	a assailli	il	assaillît
nous	avons assailli	nous	assaillissions
vous	avez assailli	vous	assaillissiez
ils	ont assailli	ils	assaillissent

CONSTRUCTIONS
on l'a assailli de questions   he was bombarded with
questions

8 s'asseoir

to sit down

PRESENT PARTICIPLE
s'asseyant

PAST PARTICIPLE
assis

PRESENT

je	m'assieds
tu	t'assieds
il	s'assied
nous	nous asseyons
vous	vous asseyez
ils	s'asseyent

ALTERNATIVE FORM OF PRESENT

je	m'assois
tu	t'assois
il	s'assoit
nous	nous assoyons
vous	vous assoyez
ils	s'assoient

IMPERATIVE

assieds-toi
asseyons-nous
asseyez-vous

IMPERFECT

je	m'asseyais
tu	t'asseyais
il	s'asseyait
nous	nous asseyions
vous	vous asseyiez
ils	s'asseyaient

FUTURE

je	m'assiérai
tu	t'assiéras
il	s'assiéra
nous	nous assiérons
vous	vous assiérez
ils	s'assiéront

CONDITIONAL

je	m'assiérais
tu	t'assiérais
il	s'assiérait
nous	nous assiérions
vous	vous assiériez
ils	s'assiéraient

PAST HISTORIC

je	m'assis
tu	t'assis
il	s'assit
nous	nous assîmes
vous	vous assîtes
ils	s'assirent

PERFECT

je	me suis assis
tu	t'es assis
il	s'est assis
nous	nous sommes assis
vous	vous êtes assis
ils	se sont assis

PRESENT SUBJUNCTIVE

je	m'asseye
tu	t'asseyes
il	s'asseye
nous	nous asseyions
vous	vous asseyiez
ils	s'asseyent

PAST SUBJUNCTIVE

je	m'assisse
tu	t'assisses
il	s'assît
nous	nous assissions
vous	vous assissiez
ils	s'assissent

CONSTRUCTIONS

veuillez vous asseoir please be seated
il s'est assis sur une chaise/par terre he sat (down) on a chair/the floor
il est assis sur une chaise/par terre he is sitting on a chair/the floor

9 attendre

to wait

PRESENT PARTICIPLE
attendant

PAST PARTICIPLE
attendu

PRESENT		IMPERFECT	
j'	attends	j'	attendais
tu	attends	tu	attendais
il	attend	il	attendait
nous	attendons	nous	attendions
vous	attendez	vous	attendiez
ils	attendent	ils	attendaient

		FUTURE	
		j'	attendrai
		tu	attendras
		il	attendra
		nous	attendrons
		vous	attendrez
		ils	attendront

IMPERATIVE		CONDITIONAL	
	attends	j'	attendrais
	attendons	tu	attendrais
	attendez	il	attendrait
		nous	attendrions
		vous	attendriez
		ils	attendraient

PAST HISTORIC		PRESENT SUBJUNCTIVE	
j'	attendis	j'	attende
tu	attendis	tu	attendes
il	attendit	il	attende
nous	attendîmes	nous	attendions
vous	attendîtes	vous	attendiez
ils	attendirent	ils	attendent

PERFECT		PAST SUBJUNCTIVE	
j'	ai attendu	j'	attendisse
tu	as attendu	tu	attendisses
il	a attendu	il	attendît
nous	avons attendu	nous	attendissions
vous	avez attendu	vous	attendissiez
ils	ont attendu	ils	attendissent

CONSTRUCTIONS
nous attendons qu'il parte we're waiting for him to leave
j'ai attendu 2 heures I waited (for) 2 hours
attends d'être plus grand wait till you're older
attendre qch de qn/qch to expect sth of sb/sth
s'attendre à qch/à faire to expect sth/to do

10 avoir
to have

PRESENT PARTICIPLE
ayant

PAST PARTICIPLE
eu

PRESENT
j'	ai
tu	as
il	a
nous	avons
vous	avez
ils	ont

IMPERATIVE
aie
ayons
ayez

IMPERFECT
j'	avais
tu	avais
il	avait
nous	avions
vous	aviez
ils	avaient

FUTURE
j'	aurai
tu	auras
il	aura
nous	aurons
vous	aurez
ils	auront

CONDITIONAL
j'	aurais
tu	aurais
il	aurait
nous	aurions
vous	auriez
ils	auraient

to have

PAST HISTORIC		PRESENT SUBJUNCTIVE	
j'	eus	j'	aie
tu	eus	tu	aies
il	eut	il	ait
nous	eûmes	nous	ayons
vous	eûtes	vous	ayez
ils	eurent	ils	aient

PERFECT		PAST SUBJUNCTIVE	
j'	ai eu	j'	eusse
tu	as eu	tu	eusses
il	a eu	il	eût
nous	avons eu	nous	eussions
vous	avez eu	vous	eussiez
ils	ont eu	ils	eussent

CONSTRUCTIONS

j'ai des lettres à écrire I've got letters to write
quel âge avez-vous? – j'ai 10 ans how old are you? – I'm 10 (years old)
avoir faim/chaud/tort to be hungry/hot/wrong
il y a there is; there are
il y a 10 ans 10 years ago

11 battre

to beat

PRESENT PARTICIPLE
battant

PAST PARTICIPLE
battu

also **abattre**
to pull down

combattre
to fight

débattre
to discuss

	PRESENT		IMPERFECT
je	bats	je	battais
tu	bats	tu	battais
il	bat	il	battait
nous	battons	nous	battions
vous	battez	vous	battiez
ils	battent	ils	battaient

FUTURE

je	battrai
tu	battras
il	battra
nous	battrons
vous	battrez
ils	battront

IMPERATIVE

bats
battons
battez

CONDITIONAL

je	battrais
tu	battrais
il	battrait
nous	battrions
vous	battriez
ils	battraient

battre 11
to beat

rabattre
to pull down

PAST HISTORIC		PRESENT SUBJUNCTIVE	
je	battis	je	batte
tu	battis	tu	battes
il	battit	il	batte
nous	battîmes	nous	battions
vous	battîtes	vous	battiez
ils	battirent	ils	battent

PERFECT		PAST SUBJUNCTIVE	
j'	ai battu	je	battisse
tu	as battu	tu	battisses
il	a battu	il	battît
nous	avons battu	nous	battissions
vous	avez battu	vous	battissiez
ils	ont battu	ils	battissent

CONSTRUCTIONS
battre des mains to clap one's hands
l'oiseau battait des ailes the bird was flapping its wings
se battre to fight

12 boire

to drink

PRESENT PARTICIPLE
buvant

PAST PARTICIPLE
bu

	PRESENT		*IMPERFECT*
je	bois	je	buvais
tu	bois	tu	buvais
il	boit	il	buvait
nous	buvons	nous	buvions
vous	buvez	vous	buviez
ils	boivent	ils	buvaient

			FUTURE
		je	boirai
		tu	boiras
		il	boira
		nous	boirons
		vous	boirez
		ils	boiront

	IMPERATIVE		*CONDITIONAL*
	bois	je	boirais
	buvons	tu	boirais
	buvez	il	boirait
		nous	boirions
		vous	boiriez
		ils	boiraient

PAST HISTORIC		PRESENT SUBJUNCTIVE	
je	bus	je	boive
tu	bus	tu	boives
il	but	il	boive
nous	bûmes	nous	buvions
vous	bûtes	vous	buviez
ils	burent	ils	boivent

PERFECT		PAST SUBJUNCTIVE	
j'	ai bu	je	busse
tu	as bu	tu	busses
il	a bu	il	bût
nous	avons bu	nous	bussions
vous	avez bu	vous	bussiez
ils	ont bu	ils	bussent

CONSTRUCTIONS
boire un verre to have a drink

13 bouillir
to boil

PRESENT PARTICIPLE
bouillant

PAST PARTICIPLE
bouilli

PRESENT		*IMPERFECT*	
je	bous	je	bouillais
tu	bous	tu	bouillais
il	bout	il	bouillait
nous	bouillons	nous	bouillions
vous	bouillez	vous	bouilliez
ils	bouillent	ils	bouillaient

		FUTURE	
		je	bouillirai
		tu	bouilliras
		il	bouillira
		nous	bouillirons
		vous	bouillirez
		ils	bouilliront

IMPERATIVE		*CONDITIONAL*	
	bous	je	bouillirais
	bouillons	tu	bouillirais
	bouillez	il	bouillirait
		nous	bouillirions
		vous	bouilliriez
		ils	bouilliraient

bouillir 13

to boil

PAST HISTORIC		PRESENT SUBJUNCTIVE	
je	bouillis	je	bouille
tu	bouillis	tu	bouilles
il	bouillit	il	bouille
nous	bouillîmes	nous	bouillions
vous	bouillîtes	vous	bouilliez
ils	bouillirent	ils	bouillent

PERFECT		PAST SUBJUNCTIVE	
j'	ai bouilli	je	bouillisse
tu	as bouilli	tu	bouillisses
il	a bouilli	il	bouillît
nous	avons bouilli	nous	bouillissions
vous	avez bouilli	vous	bouillissiez
ils	ont bouilli	ils	bouillissent

CONSTRUCTIONS

faire bouillir de l'eau/des pommes de terre to boil water/potatoes

bouillir de colère/d'impatience to seethe with anger/impatience

14 clore

to shut

PRESENT PARTICIPLE
closant

PAST PARTICIPLE
clos

PRESENT		IMPERFECT	
je	clos	je	closais
tu	clos	tu	closais
il	clôt	il	closait
nous	closons	nous	closions
vous	closez	vous	closiez
ils	closent	ils	closaient
		FUTURE	
		je	clorai
		tu	cloras
		il	clora
		nous	clorons
		vous	clorez
		ils	cloront
IMPERATIVE		CONDITIONAL	
	not used	je	clorais
		tu	clorais
		il	clorait
		nous	clorions
		vous	cloriez
		ils	cloraient

PAST HISTORIC	PRESENT SUBJUNCTIVE
not used	je **close**
	tu **closes**
	il **close**
	nous **closions**
	vous **closiez**
	ils **closent**

PERFECT	PAST SUBJUNCTIVE
j' **ai clos**	*not used*
tu **as clos**	
il **a clos**	
nous **avons clos**	
vous **avez clos**	
ils **ont clos**	

CONSTRUCTIONS
le débat s'est clos sur cette remarque the discussion
ended with that remark
clore le bec à qn to shut sb up

15 commencer
to begin

also **annoncer**
to announce

PRESENT PARTICIPLE
commençant

avancer
to move forward

PAST PARTICIPLE
commencé

déplacer
to move

PRESENT		*IMPERFECT*	
je	commence	je	commençais
tu	commences	tu	commençais
il	commence	il	commençait
nous	commençons	nous	commencions
vous	commencez	vous	commenciez
ils	commencent	ils	commençaient

		FUTURE	
		je	commencerai
		tu	commenceras
		il	commencera
		nous	commencerons
		vous	commencerez
		ils	commenceront

IMPERATIVE		*CONDITIONAL*	
	commence	je	commencerais
	commençons	tu	commencerais
	commencez	il	commencerait
		nous	commencerions
		vous	commenceriez
		ils	commenceraient

effacer
to erase

to begin

lancer
to throw

PAST HISTORIC		PRESENT SUBJUNCTIVE	
je	commençai	je	commence
tu	commenças	tu	commences
il	commença	il	commence
nous	commençâmes	nous	commencions
vous	commençâtes	vous	commenciez
ils	commencèrent	ils	commencent

PERFECT		PAST SUBJUNCTIVE	
j'	ai commencé	je	commençasse
tu	as commencé	tu	commençasses
il	a commencé	il	commençât
nous	avons commencé	nous	commençassions
vous	avez commencé	vous	commençassiez
ils	ont commencé	ils	commençassent

CONSTRUCTIONS

commencer à or **de faire**   to begin to do
commencer par qch   to begin with sth
commencer par faire qch   to begin by doing sth
il commence à pleuvoir   it's beginning to rain

16 comprendre
to understand

PRESENT PARTICIPLE
comprenant

PAST PARTICIPLE
compris

PRESENT		*IMPERFECT*	
je	comprends	je	comprenais
tu	comprends	tu	comprenais
il	comprend	il	comprenait
nous	comprenons	nous	comprenions
vous	comprenez	vous	compreniez
ils	comprennent	ils	comprenaient

FUTURE

je	comprendrai
tu	comprendras
il	comprendra
nous	comprendrons
vous	comprendrez
ils	comprendront

IMPERATIVE

comprends
comprenons
comprenez

CONDITIONAL

je	comprendrais
tu	comprendrais
il	comprendrait
nous	comprendrions
vous	comprendriez
ils	comprendraient

PAST HISTORIC		PRESENT SUBJUNCTIVE	
je	compris	je	comprenne
tu	compris	tu	comprennes
il	comprit	il	comprenne
nous	comprîmes	nous	comprenions
vous	comprîtes	vous	compreniez
ils	comprirent	ils	comprennent

PERFECT		PAST SUBJUNCTIVE	
j'	ai compris	je	comprisse
tu	as compris	tu	comprisses
il	a compris	il	comprît
nous	avons compris	nous	comprissions
vous	avez compris	vous	comprissiez
ils	ont compris	ils	comprissent

CONSTRUCTIONS

la maison comprend 10 pièces the house comprises 10 rooms

mal comprendre to misunderstand

service compris service charge included

100 F y compris l'électricité *or* **l'électricité y compris** 100 F including electricity

17 conclure

to conclude

also **exclure**
to exclude

PRESENT PARTICIPLE
concluant

PAST PARTICIPLE
conclu

PRESENT		*IMPERFECT*	
je	conclus	je	concluais
tu	conclus	tu	concluais
il	conclut	il	concluait
nous	concluons	nous	concluions
vous	concluez	vous	concluiez
ils	concluent	ils	concluaient

		FUTURE	
		je	conclurai
		tu	concluras
		il	conclura
		nous	conclurons
		vous	conclurez
		ils	concluront

IMPERATIVE	*CONDITIONAL*	
conclus	je	conclurais
concluons	tu	conclurais
concluez	il	conclurait
	nous	conclurions
	vous	concluriez
	ils	concluraient

conclure 17
to conclude

PAST HISTORIC		PRESENT SUBJUNCTIVE	
je	conclus	je	conclue
tu	conclus	tu	conclues
il	conclut	il	conclue
nous	conclûmes	nous	concluions
vous	conclûtes	vous	concluiez
ils	conclurent	ils	concluent

PERFECT		PAST SUBJUNCTIVE	
j'	ai conclu	je	conclusse
tu	as conclu	tu	conclusses
il	a conclu	il	conclût
nous	avons conclu	nous	conclussions
vous	avez conclu	vous	conclussiez
ils	ont conclu	ils	conclussent

CONSTRUCTIONS
marché conclu! it's a deal!
j'en ai conclu qu'il était parti I concluded that he had gone
ils ont conclu à son innocence they concluded that he was innocent

47

18 conduire
to lead

also **éconduire**
to dismiss

PRESENT PARTICIPLE
conduisant

PAST PARTICIPLE
conduit

PRESENT		*IMPERFECT*	
je	**conduis**	je	**conduisais**
tu	**conduis**	tu	**conduisais**
il	**conduit**	il	**conduisait**
nous	**conduisons**	nous	**conduisions**
vous	**conduisez**	vous	**conduisiez**
ils	**conduisent**	ils	**conduisaient**

		FUTURE	
		je	**conduirai**
		tu	**conduiras**
		il	**conduira**
		nous	**conduirons**
		vous	**conduirez**
		ils	**conduiront**

IMPERATIVE	*CONDITIONAL*	
conduis	je	**conduirais**
conduisons	tu	**conduirais**
conduisez	il	**conduirait**
	nous	**conduirions**
	vous	**conduiriez**
	ils	**conduiraient**

conduire 18

to lead

PAST HISTORIC		PRESENT SUBJUNCTIVE	
je	conduisis	je	conduise
tu	conduisis	tu	conduises
il	conduisit	il	conduise
nous	conduisîmes	nous	conduisions
vous	conduisîtes	vous	conduisiez
ils	conduisirent	ils	conduisent

PERFECT		PAST SUBJUNCTIVE	
j'	ai conduit	je	conduisisse
tu	as conduit	tu	conduisisses
il	a conduit	il	conduisît
nous	avons conduit	nous	conduisissions
vous	avez conduit	vous	conduisissiez
ils	ont conduit	ils	conduisissent

CONSTRUCTIONS

conduire qn quelque part   to take sb somewhere; to drive sb somewhere

conduire qn à faire qch   to lead sb to do sth

cet escalier conduit au toit   these stairs lead (up) to the roof

se conduire   to behave (oneself)

19 connaître

to know

PRESENT PARTICIPLE
connaissant

PAST PARTICIPLE
connu

also **méconnaître**
to be unaware of

reconnaître
to recognize

PRESENT			*IMPERFECT*		
	je	connais		je	connaissais
	tu	connais		tu	connaissais
	il	connaît		il	connaissait
	nous	connaissons		nous	connaissions
	vous	connaissez		vous	connaissiez
	ils	connaissent		ils	connaissaient
			FUTURE		
				je	connaîtrai
				tu	connaîtras
				il	connaîtra
				nous	connaîtrons
				vous	connaîtrez
				ils	connaîtront
IMPERATIVE			*CONDITIONAL*		
		connais		je	connaîtrais
		connaissons		tu	connaîtrais
		connaissez		il	connaîtrait
				nous	connaîtrions
				vous	connaîtriez
				ils	connaîtraient

PAST HISTORIC		PRESENT SUBJUNCTIVE	
je	connus	je	connaisse
tu	connus	tu	connaisses
il	connut	il	connaisse
nous	connûmes	nous	connaissions
vous	connûtes	vous	connaissiez
ils	connurent	ils	connaissent

PERFECT		PAST SUBJUNCTIVE	
j'	ai connu	je	connusse
tu	as connu	tu	connusses
il	a connu	il	connût
nous	avons connu	nous	connussions
vous	avez connu	vous	connussiez
ils	ont connu	ils	connussent

CONSTRUCTIONS

connaître qn de vue/nom to know sb by sight/name
il connaît bien la littérature anglaise he's very familiar
with English literature
faire connaître qn à qn to introduce sb to sb
se faire connaître to make a name for oneself; to
introduce oneself

20 coudre

to sew

PRESENT PARTICIPLE
cousant

PAST PARTICIPLE
cousu

	PRESENT		IMPERFECT
je	couds	je	cousais
tu	couds	tu	cousais
il	coud	il	cousait
nous	cousons	nous	cousions
vous	cousez	vous	cousiez
ils	cousent	ils	cousaient

FUTURE

je	coudrai
tu	coudras
il	coudra
nous	coudrons
vous	coudrez
ils	coudront

IMPERATIVE

couds
cousons
cousez

CONDITIONAL

je	coudrais
tu	coudrais
il	coudrait
nous	coudrions
vous	coudriez
ils	coudraient

PAST HISTORIC		PRESENT SUBJUNCTIVE	
je	cousis	je	couse
tu	cousis	tu	couses
il	cousit	il	couse
nous	cousîmes	nous	cousions
vous	cousîtes	vous	cousiez
ils	cousirent	ils	cousent

PERFECT		PAST SUBJUNCTIVE	
j'	ai cousu	je	cousisse
tu	as cousu	tu	cousisses
il	a cousu	il	cousît
nous	avons cousu	nous	cousissions
vous	avez cousu	vous	cousissiez
ils	ont cousu	ils	cousissent

CONSTRUCTIONS

coudre un bouton à une veste   to sew a button on a
jacket

21 courir

to run

also **accourir**
to rush

PRESENT PARTICIPLE
courant

concourir
to compete

PAST PARTICIPLE
couru

parcourir
to go through

PRESENT

je	cours
tu	cours
il	court
nous	courons
vous	courez
ils	courent

IMPERFECT

je	courais
tu	courais
il	courait
nous	courions
vous	couriez
ils	couraient

FUTURE

je	courrai
tu	courras
il	courra
nous	courrons
vous	courrez
ils	courront

IMPERATIVE

cours
courons
courez

CONDITIONAL

je	courrais
tu	courrais
il	courrait
nous	courrions
vous	courriez
ils	courraient

secourir
to rescue

to run

PAST HISTORIC		PRESENT SUBJUNCTIVE	
je	courus	je	coure
tu	courus	tu	coures
il	courut	il	coure
nous	courûmes	nous	courions
vous	courûtes	vous	couriez
ils	coururent	ils	courent
PERFECT		PAST SUBJUNCTIVE	
j'	ai couru	je	courusse
tu	as couru	tu	courusses
il	a couru	il	courût
nous	avons couru	nous	courussions
vous	avez couru	vous	courussiez
ils	ont couru	ils	courussent

CONSTRUCTIONS

courir faire qch   to rush and do sth
courir à toutes jambes   to run as fast as one's legs can carry one
le bruit court que ...   the rumour is going round that ...
courir le risque de   to run the risk of

22 couvrir

to cover

also **recouvrir**
to re-cover

PRESENT PARTICIPLE
couvrant

PAST PARTICIPLE
couvert

PRESENT		*IMPERFECT*	
je	couvre	je	couvrais
tu	couvres	tu	couvrais
il	couvre	il	couvrait
nous	couvrons	nous	couvrions
vous	couvrez	vous	couvriez
ils	couvrent	ils	couvraient

FUTURE

je	couvrirai
tu	couvriras
il	couvrira
nous	couvrirons
vous	couvrirez
ils	couvriront

IMPERATIVE

couvre
couvrons
couvrez

CONDITIONAL

je	couvrirais
tu	couvrirais
il	couvrirait
nous	couvririons
vous	couvririez
ils	couvriraient

PAST HISTORIC		PRESENT SUBJUNCTIVE	
je	couvris	je	couvre
tu	couvris	tu	couvres
il	couvrit	il	couvre
nous	couvrîmes	nous	couvrions
vous	couvrîtes	vous	couvriez
ils	couvrirent	ils	couvrent

PERFECT		PAST SUBJUNCTIVE	
j'	ai couvert	je	couvrisse
tu	as couvert	tu	couvrisses
il	a couvert	il	couvrît
nous	avons couvert	nous	couvrissions
vous	avez couvert	vous	couvrissiez
ils	ont couvert	ils	couvrissent

CONSTRUCTIONS

la voiture nous a couverts de boue   the car covered us in mud

couvrir qn de cadeaux   to shower sb with gifts

elle s'est couvert le visage des mains   she covered her face with her hands

couvrez-vous bien!   wrap up well!

23 craindre
to fear

also **contraindre**
to compel

PRESENT PARTICIPLE
craignant

plaindre
to pity

PAST PARTICIPLE
craint

PRESENT		IMPERFECT	
je	crains	je	craignais
tu	crains	tu	craignais
il	craint	il	craignait
nous	craignons	nous	craignions
vous	craignez	vous	craigniez
ils	craignent	ils	craignaient

		FUTURE	
		je	craindrai
		tu	craindras
		il	craindra
		nous	craindrons
		vous	craindrez
		ils	craindront

IMPERATIVE	CONDITIONAL	
crains	je	craindrais
craignons	tu	craindrais
craignez	il	craindrait
	nous	craindrions
	vous	craindriez
	ils	craindraient

to fear

PAST HISTORIC		PRESENT SUBJUNCTIVE	
je	craignis	je	craigne
tu	craignis	tu	craignes
il	craignit	il	craigne
nous	craignîmes	nous	craignions
vous	craignîtes	vous	craigniez
ils	craignirent	ils	craignent

PERFECT		PAST SUBJUNCTIVE	
j'	ai craint	je	craignisse
tu	as craint	tu	craignisses
il	a craint	il	craignît
nous	avons craint	nous	craignissions
vous	avez craint	vous	craignissiez
ils	ont craint	ils	craignissent

CONSTRUCTIONS
ne craignez rien don't be afraid
craindre de faire qch to be afraid of doing sth
ces plantes craignent la chaleur these plants dislike heat

24 créer

to create

also **agréer**
to accept

maugréer
to grumble

procréer
to procreate

PRESENT PARTICIPLE
créant

PAST PARTICIPLE
créé

PRESENT		IMPERFECT	
je	crée	je	créais
tu	crées	tu	créais
il	crée	il	créait
nous	créons	nous	créions
vous	créez	vous	créiez
ils	créent	ils	créaient

		FUTURE	
		je	créerai
		tu	créeras
		il	créera
		nous	créerons
		vous	créerez
		ils	créeront

IMPERATIVE	CONDITIONAL	
crée	je	créerais
créons	tu	créerais
créez	il	créerait
	nous	créerions
	vous	créeriez
	ils	créeraient

récréer
to recreate

PAST HISTORIC		PRESENT SUBJUNCTIVE	
je	créai	je	crée
tu	créas	tu	crées
il	créa	il	crée
nous	créâmes	nous	créions
vous	créâtes	vous	créiez
ils	créèrent	ils	créent

PERFECT		PAST SUBJUNCTIVE	
j'	ai créé	je	créasse
tu	as créé	tu	créasses
il	a créé	il	créât
nous	avons créé	nous	créassions
vous	avez créé	vous	créassiez
ils	ont créé	ils	créassent

CONSTRUCTIONS
il nous a créé des ennuis he's caused us problems
il s'est créé une clientèle he has built up custom

25 crier

to shout

also **amplifier**
to amplify

PRESENT PARTICIPLE
criant

associer
to associate

PAST PARTICIPLE
crié

copier
to copy

PRESENT		*IMPERFECT*	
je	crie	je	criais
tu	cries	tu	criais
il	crie	il	criait
nous	crions	nous	criions
vous	criez	vous	criiez
ils	crient	ils	criaient

		FUTURE	
		je	crierai
		tu	crieras
		il	criera
		nous	crierons
		vous	crierez
		ils	crieront

IMPERATIVE		*CONDITIONAL*	
	crie	je	crierais
	crions	tu	crierais
	criez	il	crierait
		nous	crierions
		vous	crieriez
		ils	crieraient

étudier
to study

marier
to marry

PAST HISTORIC		PRESENT SUBJUNCTIVE	
je	criai	je	crie
tu	crias	tu	cries
il	cria	il	crie
nous	criâmes	nous	criions
vous	criâtes	vous	criiez
ils	crièrent	ils	crient

PERFECT		PAST SUBJUNCTIVE	
j'	ai crié	je	criasse
tu	as crié	tu	criasses
il	a crié	il	criât
nous	avons crié	nous	criassions
vous	avez crié	vous	criassiez
ils	ont crié	ils	criassent

CONSTRUCTIONS
crier à tue-tête to shout one's head off
crier contre *or* **après qn** to nag (at) sb
crier à qn de faire qch to shout at sb to do sth
crier qch sur les toits to proclaim sth from the rooftops
crier au secours to shout for help

26 croire

to believe

PRESENT PARTICIPLE
croyant

PAST PARTICIPLE
cru

PRESENT		*IMPERFECT*	
je	crois	je	croyais
tu	crois	tu	croyais
il	croit	il	croyait
nous	croyons	nous	croyions
vous	croyez	vous	croyiez
ils	croient	ils	croyaient

		FUTURE	
		je	croirai
		tu	croiras
		il	croira
		nous	croirons
		vous	croirez
		ils	croiront

IMPERATIVE		*CONDITIONAL*	
	crois	je	croirais
	croyons	tu	croirais
	croyez	il	croirait
		nous	croirions
		vous	croiriez
		ils	croiraient

PAST HISTORIC		PRESENT SUBJUNCTIVE	
je	crus	je	croie
tu	crus	tu	croies
il	crut	il	croie
nous	crûmes	nous	croyions
vous	crûtes	vous	croyiez
ils	crurent	ils	croient

PERFECT		PAST SUBJUNCTIVE	
j'	ai cru	je	crusse
tu	as cru	tu	crusses
il	a cru	il	crût
nous	avons cru	nous	crussions
vous	avez cru	vous	crussiez
ils	ont cru	ils	crussent

CONSTRUCTIONS
croire aux fantômes/en Dieu to believe in ghosts/God
on l'a cru mort he was presumed (to be) dead
elle croyait avoir perdu son sac she thought she had lost her bag
je crois que oui I think so, I think we will *etc*

27 croître

to grow

PRESENT PARTICIPLE
croissant

PAST PARTICIPLE
crû (*NB*: **crue, crus, crues**)

PRESENT		*IMPERFECT*	
je	**crois**	je	**croissais**
tu	**crois**	tu	**croissais**
il	**croît**	il	**croissait**
nous	**croissons**	nous	**croissions**
vous	**croissez**	vous	**croissiez**
ils	**croissent**	ils	**croissaient**

		FUTURE	
		je	**croîtrai**
		tu	**croîtras**
		il	**croîtra**
		nous	**croîtrons**
		vous	**croîtrez**
		ils	**croîtront**

IMPERATIVE	*CONDITIONAL*	
crois	je	**croîtrais**
croissons	tu	**croîtrais**
croissez	il	**croîtrait**
	nous	**croîtrions**
	vous	**croîtriez**
	ils	**croîtraient**

PAST HISTORIC		PRESENT SUBJUNCTIVE	
je	crûs	je	croisse
tu	crûs	tu	croisses
il	crût	il	croisse
nous	crûmes	nous	croissions
vous	crûtes	vous	croissiez
ils	crûrent	ils	croissent

PERFECT		PAST SUBJUNCTIVE	
j'	ai crû	je	crûsse
tu	as crû	tu	crûsses
il	a crû	il	crût
nous	avons crû	nous	crûssions
vous	avez crû	vous	crûssiez
ils	ont crû	ils	crûssent

CONSTRUCTIONS
croître en beauté/nombre to grow in beauty/number
les jours croissent the days are getting longer

28 cueillir

to pick

also **accueillir**
to welcome

PRESENT PARTICIPLE
cueillant

recueillir
to collect

PAST PARTICIPLE
cueilli

PRESENT		*IMPERFECT*	
je	cueille	je	cueillais
tu	cueilles	tu	cueillais
il	cueille	il	cueillait
nous	cueillons	nous	cueillions
vous	cueillez	vous	cueilliez
ils	cueillent	ils	cueillaient

		FUTURE	
		je	cueillerai
		tu	cueilleras
		il	cueillera
		nous	cueillerons
		vous	cueillerez
		ils	cueilleront

IMPERATIVE		*CONDITIONAL*	
	cueille	je	cueillerais
	cueillons	tu	cueillerais
	cueillez	il	cueillerait
		nous	cueillerions
		vous	cueilleriez
		ils	cueilleraient

cueillir 28
to pick

PAST HISTORIC		PRESENT SUBJUNCTIVE	
je	cueillis	je	cueille
tu	cueillis	tu	cueilles
il	cueillit	il	cueille
nous	cueillîmes	nous	cueillions
vous	cueillîtes	vous	cueilliez
ils	cueillirent	ils	cueillent

PERFECT		PAST SUBJUNCTIVE	
j'	ai cueilli	je	cueillisse
tu	as cueilli	tu	cueillisses
il	a cueilli	il	cueillît
nous	avons cueilli	nous	cueillissions
vous	avez cueilli	vous	cueillissiez
ils	ont cueilli	ils	cueillissent

CONSTRUCTIONS
cueillir qn à froid   to catch sb off guard

29 cuire
to cook

also **construire**
to build

PRESENT PARTICIPLE
cuisant

instruire
to teach

PAST PARTICIPLE
cuit

produire
to produce

PRESENT		IMPERFECT	
je	cuis	je	cuisais
tu	cuis	tu	cuisais
il	cuit	il	cuisait
nous	cuisons	nous	cuisions
vous	cuisez	vous	cuisiez
ils	cuisent	ils	cuisaient

		FUTURE	
		je	cuirai
		tu	cuiras
		il	cuira
		nous	cuirons
		vous	cuirez
		ils	cuiront

IMPERATIVE		CONDITIONAL	
	cuis	je	cuirais
	cuisons	tu	cuirais
	cuisez	il	cuirait
		nous	cuirions
		vous	cuiriez
		ils	cuiraient

réduire
to reduce

séduire
to charm

PAST HISTORIC		PRESENT SUBJUNCTIVE	
je	cuisis	je	cuise
tu	cuisis	tu	cuises
il	cuisit	il	cuise
nous	cuisîmes	nous	cuisions
vous	cuisîtes	vous	cuisiez
ils	cuisirent	ils	cuisent
PERFECT		PAST SUBJUNCTIVE	
j'	ai cuit	je	cuisisse
tu	as cuit	tu	cuisisses
il	a cuit	il	cuisît
nous	avons cuit	nous	cuisissions
vous	avez cuit	vous	cuisissiez
ils	ont cuit	ils	cuisissent

CONSTRUCTIONS
cuire au gaz/à l'électricité to cook with gas/by
electricity
cuire au four to bake; to roast
cuire à la vapeur to steam
cuire à feu doux to cook gently
bien cuit well done

30 découvrir

to discover

PRESENT PARTICIPLE
découvrant

PAST PARTICIPLE
découvert

PRESENT		IMPERFECT	
je	découvre	je	découvrais
tu	découvres	tu	découvrais
il	découvre	il	découvrait
nous	découvrons	nous	découvrions
vous	découvrez	vous	découvriez
ils	découvrent	ils	découvraient

		FUTURE	
		je	découvrirai
		tu	découvriras
		il	découvrira
		nous	découvrirons
		vous	découvrirez
		ils	découvriront

IMPERATIVE		CONDITIONAL	
	découvre	je	découvrirais
	découvrons	tu	découvrirais
	découvrez	il	découvrirait
		nous	découvririons
		vous	découvririez
		ils	découvriraient

to discover

PAST HISTORIC		PRESENT SUBJUNCTIVE	
je	découvris	je	découvre
tu	découvris	tu	découvres
il	découvrit	il	découvre
nous	découvrîmes	nous	découvrions
vous	découvrîtes	vous	découvriez
ils	découvrirent	ils	découvrent

PERFECT		PAST SUBJUNCTIVE	
j'	ai découvert	je	découvrisse
tu	as découvert	tu	découvrisses
il	a découvert	il	découvrît
nous	avons découvert	nous	découvrissions
vous	avez découvert	vous	découvrissiez
ils	ont découvert	ils	découvrissent

CONSTRUCTIONS

il craint d'être découvert   he's afraid of being found out
une robe qui découvre les épaules   a dress which reveals
the shoulders
se découvrir   to take off one's hat; to undress

31 descendre

to go down

PRESENT PARTICIPLE
descendant

PAST PARTICIPLE
descendu

PRESENT		*IMPERFECT*	
je	descends	je	descendais
tu	descends	tu	descendais
il	descend	il	descendait
nous	descendons	nous	descendions
vous	descendez	vous	descendiez
ils	descendent	ils	descendaient

		FUTURE	
		je	descendrai
		tu	descendras
		il	descendra
		nous	descendrons
		vous	descendrez
		ils	descendront

IMPERATIVE		*CONDITIONAL*	
	descends	je	descendrais
	descendons	tu	descendrais
	descendez	il	descendrait
		nous	descendrions
		vous	descendriez
		ils	descendraient

to go down

PAST HISTORIC		PRESENT SUBJUNCTIVE	
je	descendis	je	descende
tu	descendis	tu	descendes
il	descendit	il	descende
nous	descendîmes	nous	descendions
vous	descendîtes	vous	descendiez
ils	descendirent	ils	descendent

PERFECT		PAST SUBJUNCTIVE	
je	suis descendu	je	descendisse
tu	es descendu	tu	descendisses
il	est descendu	il	descendît
nous	sommes descendus	nous	descendissions
vous	êtes descendu(s)	vous	descendissiez
ils	sont descendus	ils	descendissent

CONSTRUCTIONS

descendre de voiture/du train/de bicyclette   to get out of the car/off the train/off one's bicycle

sa jupe lui descend jusqu'aux chevilles   her skirt comes down to her ankles

il a descendu la valise   he took the case down

32 détruire
to destroy

PRESENT PARTICIPLE
détruisant

PAST PARTICIPLE
détruit

PRESENT		IMPERFECT	
je	**détruis**	je	**détruisais**
tu	**détruis**	tu	**détruisais**
il	**détruit**	il	**détruisait**
nous	**détruisons**	nous	**détruisions**
vous	**détruisez**	vous	**détruisiez**
ils	**détruisent**	ils	**détruisaient**

FUTURE

je	**détruirai**
tu	**détruiras**
il	**détruira**
nous	**détruirons**
vous	**détruirez**
ils	**détruiront**

IMPERATIVE	CONDITIONAL	
détruis	je	**détruirais**
détruisons	tu	**détruirais**
détruisez	il	**détruirait**
	nous	**détruirions**
	vous	**détruiriez**
	ils	**détruiraient**

PAST HISTORIC		PRESENT SUBJUNCTIVE	
je	détruisis	je	détruise
tu	détruisis	tu	détruises
il	détruisit	il	détruise
nous	détruisîmes	nous	détruisions
vous	détruisîtes	vous	détruisiez
ils	détruisirent	ils	détruisent

PERFECT		PAST SUBJUNCTIVE	
j'	ai détruit	je	détruisisse
tu	as détruit	tu	détruisisses
il	a détruit	il	détruisît
nous	avons détruit	nous	détruisissions
vous	avez détruit	vous	détruisissiez
ils	ont détruit	ils	détruisissent

CONSTRUCTIONS
détruire par le feu to destroy by fire

33 devenir
to become

PRESENT PARTICIPLE
devenant

PAST PARTICIPLE
devenu

PRESENT		*IMPERFECT*	
je	**deviens**	je	**devenais**
tu	**deviens**	tu	**devenais**
il	**devient**	il	**devenait**
nous	**devenons**	nous	**devenions**
vous	**devenez**	vous	**deveniez**
ils	**deviennent**	ils	**devenaient**

		FUTURE	
		je	**deviendrai**
		tu	**deviendras**
		il	**deviendra**
		nous	**deviendrons**
		vous	**deviendrez**
		ils	**deviendront**

IMPERATIVE		*CONDITIONAL*	
	deviens	je	**deviendrais**
	devenons	tu	**deviendrais**
	devenez	il	**deviendrait**
		nous	**deviendrions**
		vous	**deviendriez**
		ils	**deviendraient**

PAST HISTORIC		PRESENT SUBJUNCTIVE	
je	devins	je	devienne
tu	devins	tu	deviennes
il	devint	il	devienne
nous	devînmes	nous	devenions
vous	devîntes	vous	deveniez
ils	devinrent	ils	deviennent

PERFECT		PAST SUBJUNCTIVE	
je	suis devenu	je	devinsse
tu	es devenu	tu	devinsses
il	est devenu	il	devînt
nous	sommes devenus	nous	devinssions
vous	êtes devenu(s)	vous	devinssiez
ils	sont devenus	ils	devinssent

CONSTRUCTIONS

devenir médecin/professeur   to become a doctor/a teacher

devenir vieux/grand   to get old/tall

qu'est-il devenu?   what has become of him?

il devient de plus en plus agressif   he's growing increasingly aggressive

34 devoir

to have to; to owe

PRESENT PARTICIPLE
devant

PAST PARTICIPLE
dû (*NB*: **due, dus, dues**)

PRESENT		*IMPERFECT*	
je	**dois**	je	**devais**
tu	**dois**	tu	**devais**
il	**doit**	il	**devait**
nous	**devons**	nous	**devions**
vous	**devez**	vous	**deviez**
ils	**doivent**	ils	**devaient**

		FUTURE	
		je	**devrai**
		tu	**devras**
		il	**devra**
		nous	**devrons**
		vous	**devrez**
		ils	**devront**

IMPERATIVE		*CONDITIONAL*	
	dois	je	**devrais**
	devons	tu	**devrais**
	devez	il	**devrait**
		nous	**devrions**
		vous	**devriez**
		ils	**devraient**

devoir 34

to have to; to owe

PAST HISTORIC		PRESENT SUBJUNCTIVE	
je	dus	je	doive
tu	dus	tu	doives
il	dut	il	doive
nous	dûmes	nous	devions
vous	dûtes	vous	deviez
ils	dûrent	ils	doivent

PERFECT		PAST SUBJUNCTIVE	
j'	ai dû	je	dusse
tu	as dû	tu	dusses
il	a dû	il	dût
nous	avons dû	nous	dussions
vous	avez dû	vous	dussiez
ils	ont dû	ils	dussent

CONSTRUCTIONS

devoir qch à qn to owe sb sth
devoir faire qch to have to do sth
il doit arriver ce soir he is due (to arrive) tonight
il a dû s'égarer he must have got lost
ceci est dû à ... this is due to ...

35 dire

to say

PRESENT PARTICIPLE
disant

PAST PARTICIPLE
dit

PRESENT		IMPERFECT	
je	dis	je	disais
tu	dis	tu	disais
il	dit	il	disait
nous	disons	nous	disions
vous	dites	vous	disiez
ils	disent	ils	disaient

		FUTURE	
		je	dirai
		tu	diras
		il	dira
		nous	dirons
		vous	direz
		ils	diront

IMPERATIVE		CONDITIONAL	
	dis	je	dirais
	disons	tu	dirais
	dites	il	dirait
		nous	dirions
		vous	diriez
		ils	diraient

PAST HISTORIC		PRESENT SUBJUNCTIVE	
je	dis	je	dise
tu	dis	tu	dises
il	dit	il	dise
nous	dîmes	nous	disions
vous	dîtes	vous	disiez
ils	dirent	ils	disent

PERFECT		PAST SUBJUNCTIVE	
j'	ai dit	je	disse
tu	as dit	tu	disses
il	a dit	il	dît
nous	avons dit	nous	dissions
vous	avez dit	vous	dissiez
ils	ont dit	ils	dissent

CONSTRUCTIONS
dire qch à qn to tell sb sth
dire à qn de faire qch to tell sb to do sth
cela ne me dit rien I don't fancy it
on dirait du poulet it tastes like chicken
on dirait Jean it looks like John

36 donner

to give

also **accepter**
to accept

PRESENT PARTICIPLE
donnant

causer
to cause

PAST PARTICIPLE
donné

laver
to wash

PRESENT		IMPERFECT	
je	donne	je	donnais
tu	donnes	tu	donnais
il	donne	il	donnait
nous	donnons	nous	donnions
vous	donnez	vous	donniez
ils	donnent	ils	donnaient

FUTURE

je	donnerai
tu	donneras
il	donnera
nous	donnerons
vous	donnerez
ils	donneront

IMPERATIVE	CONDITIONAL	
donne	je	donnerais
donnons	tu	donnerais
donnez	il	donnerait
	nous	donnerions
	vous	donneriez
	ils	donneraient

poser
to put

rêver
to dream

PAST HISTORIC		PRESENT SUBJUNCTIVE	
je	donnai	je	donne
tu	donnas	tu	donnes
il	donna	il	donne
nous	donnâmes	nous	donnions
vous	donnâtes	vous	donniez
ils	donnèrent	ils	donnent
PERFECT		PAST SUBJUNCTIVE	
j'	ai donné	je	donnasse
tu	as donné	tu	donnasses
il	a donné	il	donnât
nous	avons donné	nous	donnassions
vous	avez donné	vous	donnassiez
ils	ont donné	ils	donnassent

CONSTRUCTIONS
donner qch à qn to give sb sth
donner quelque chose à faire à qn to give sb something to do
donner à boire à qn to give sb something to drink
cela me donne soif this makes me (feel) thirsty
donner sur to open onto; to overlook

37 dormir
to sleep

also **s'endormir**
to fall asleep

PRESENT PARTICIPLE
dormant

PAST PARTICIPLE
dormi

PRESENT		*IMPERFECT*	
je	**dors**	je	**dormais**
tu	**dors**	tu	**dormais**
il	**dort**	il	**dormait**
nous	**dormons**	nous	**dormions**
vous	**dormez**	vous	**dormiez**
ils	**dorment**	ils	**dormaient**

		FUTURE	
		je	**dormirai**
		tu	**dormiras**
		il	**dormira**
		nous	**dormirons**
		vous	**dormirez**
		ils	**dormiront**

IMPERATIVE		*CONDITIONAL*	
	dors	je	**dormirais**
	dormons	tu	**dormirais**
	dormez	il	**dormirait**
		nous	**dormirions**
		vous	**dormiriez**
		ils	**dormiraient**

PAST HISTORIC		PRESENT SUBJUNCTIVE	
je	dormis	je	dorme
tu	dormis	tu	dormes
il	dormit	il	dorme
nous	dormîmes	nous	dormions
vous	dormîtes	vous	dormiez
ils	dormirent	ils	dorment

PERFECT		PAST SUBJUNCTIVE	
j'	ai dormi	je	dormisse
tu	as dormi	tu	dormisses
il	a dormi	il	dormît
nous	avons dormi	nous	dormissions
vous	avez dormi	vous	dormissiez
ils	ont dormi	ils	dormissent

CONSTRUCTIONS

il dort he's asleep
j'ai mal dormi I didn't sleep well
il dort d'un sommeil léger he's a light sleeper
je n'ai pas dormi de la nuit I didn't sleep a wink (all night)

38 écrire
to write

also **décrire**
to describe

PRESENT PARTICIPLE
écrivant

inscrire
to write

PAST PARTICIPLE
écrit

souscrire
to subscribe

PRESENT		*IMPERFECT*	
j'	écris	j'	écrivais
tu	écris	tu	écrivais
il	écrit	il	écrivait
nous	écrivons	nous	écrivions
vous	écrivez	vous	écriviez
ils	écrivent	ils	écrivaient

		FUTURE	
		j'	écrirai
		tu	écriras
		il	écrira
		nous	écrirons
		vous	écrirez
		ils	écriront

IMPERATIVE		*CONDITIONAL*	
	écris	j'	écrirais
	écrivons	tu	écrirais
	écrivez	il	écrirait
		nous	écririons
		vous	écririez
		ils	écriraient

to write

transcrire
to transcribe

PAST HISTORIC

j'	écrivis
tu	écrivis
il	écrivit
nous	écrivîmes
vous	écrivîtes
ils	écrivirent

PERFECT

j'	ai écrit
tu	as écrit
il	a écrit
nous	avons écrit
vous	avez écrit
ils	ont écrit

PRESENT SUBJUNCTIVE

j'	écrive
tu	écrives
il	écrive
nous	écrivions
vous	écriviez
ils	écrivent

PAST SUBJUNCTIVE

j'	écrivisse
tu	écrivisses
il	écrivît
nous	écrivissions
vous	écrivissiez
ils	écrivissent

CONSTRUCTIONS

écrit à la main/à la machine   handwritten/typed
appeler s'écrit avec deux p   appeler is spelt with two ps

39 entrer

to enter

PRESENT PARTICIPLE
entrant

PAST PARTICIPLE
entré

PRESENT		*IMPERFECT*	
j'	entre	j'	entrais
tu	entres	tu	entrais
il	entre	il	entrait
nous	entrons	nous	entrions
vous	entrez	vous	entriez
ils	entrent	ils	entraient

		FUTURE	
		j'	entrerai
		tu	entreras
		il	entrera
		nous	entrerons
		vous	entrerez
		ils	entreront

IMPERATIVE		*CONDITIONAL*	
	entre	j'	entrerais
	entrons	tu	entrerais
	entrez	il	entrerait
		nous	entrerions
		vous	entreriez
		ils	entreraient

PAST HISTORIC		PRESENT SUBJUNCTIVE	
j'	entrai	j'	entre
tu	entras	tu	entres
il	entra	il	entre
nous	entrâmes	nous	entrions
vous	entrâtes	vous	entriez
ils	entrèrent	ils	entrent

PERFECT		PAST SUBJUNCTIVE	
je	suis entré	j'	entrasse
tu	es entré	tu	entrasses
il	est entré	il	entrât
nous	sommes entrés	nous	entrassions
vous	êtes entré(s)	vous	entrassiez
ils	sont entrés	ils	entrassent

CONSTRUCTIONS

entrer dans une pièce/une voiture   to go (*or* come) into a room/get into a car
faire entrer qn   to show *or* ask sb in
entrer dans un club/une firme   to join a club/firm
ça n'entre pas dans ce tiroir   it won't go into this drawer

40 envoyer

to send *also* **renvoyer**

to send back

PRESENT PARTICIPLE
envoyant

PAST PARTICIPLE
envoyé

PRESENT		*IMPERFECT*	
j'	envoie	j'	envoyais
tu	envoies	tu	envoyais
il	envoie	il	envoyait
nous	envoyons	nous	envoyions
vous	envoyez	vous	envoyiez
ils	envoient	ils	envoyaient

FUTURE	
j'	enverrai
tu	enverras
il	enverra
nous	enverrons
vous	enverrez
ils	enverront

IMPERATIVE		*CONDITIONAL*	
	envoie	j'	enverrais
	envoyons	tu	enverrais
	envoyez	il	enverrait
		nous	enverrions
		vous	enverriez
		ils	enverraient

PAST HISTORIC		PRESENT SUBJUNCTIVE	
j'	envoyai	j'	envoie
tu	envoyas	tu	envoies
il	envoya	il	envoie
nous	envoyâmes	nous	envoyions
vous	envoyâtes	vous	envoyiez
ils	envoyèrent	ils	envoient

PERFECT		PAST SUBJUNCTIVE	
j'	ai envoyé	j'	envoyasse
tu	as envoyé	tu	envoyasses
il	a envoyé	il	envoyât
nous	avons envoyé	nous	envoyassions
vous	avez envoyé	vous	envoyassiez
ils	ont envoyé	ils	envoyassent

CONSTRUCTIONS
envoyer chercher qn/qch   to send for sb/sth

41 espérer
to hope

PRESENT PARTICIPLE
espérant

PAST PARTICIPLE
espéré

also **accélérer**
to accelerate

céder
to give up

compléter
to complete

	PRESENT		IMPERFECT
j'	espère	j'	espérais
tu	espères	tu	espérais
il	espère	il	espérait
nous	espérons	nous	espérions
vous	espérez	vous	espériez
ils	espèrent	ils	espéraient

FUTURE

j'	espérerai
tu	espéreras
il	espérera
nous	espérerons
vous	espérerez
ils	espéreront

	IMPERATIVE		CONDITIONAL
	espère	j'	espérerais
	espérons	tu	espérerais
	espérez	il	espérerait
		nous	espérerions
		vous	espéreriez
		ils	espéreraient

to hope

régler
to settle

sécher
to dry

PAST HISTORIC		PRESENT SUBJUNCTIVE	
j'	espérai	j'	espère
tu	espéras	tu	espères
il	espéra	il	espère
nous	espérâmes	nous	espérions
vous	espérâtes	vous	espériez
ils	espérèrent	ils	espèrent

PERFECT		PAST SUBJUNCTIVE	
j'	ai espéré	j'	espérasse
tu	as espéré	tu	espérasses
il	a espéré	il	espérât
nous	avons espéré	nous	espérassions
vous	avez espéré	vous	espérassiez
ils	ont espéré	ils	espérassent

CONSTRUCTIONS

espérer faire qch to hope to do sth
viendra-t-il? – je l'espère (bien) will he come? – I
(certainly) hope so
j'espère bien n'avoir rien oublié I hope I haven't
forgotten anything

42 être
to be

PRESENT PARTICIPLE
étant

PAST PARTICIPLE
été

PRESENT		*IMPERFECT*	
je	**suis**	j'	**étais**
tu	**es**	tu	**étais**
il	**est**	il	**était**
nous	**sommes**	nous	**étions**
vous	**êtes**	vous	**étiez**
ils	**sont**	ils	**étaient**

		FUTURE	
		je	**serai**
		tu	**seras**
		il	**sera**
		nous	**serons**
		vous	**serez**
		ils	**seront**

IMPERATIVE	*CONDITIONAL*	
sois	je	**serais**
soyons	tu	**serais**
soyez	il	**serait**
	nous	**serions**
	vous	**seriez**
	ils	**seraient**

PAST HISTORIC		PRESENT SUBJUNCTIVE	
je	fus	je	sois
tu	fus	tu	sois
il	fut	il	soit
nous	fûmes	nous	soyons
vous	fûtes	vous	soyez
ils	furent	ils	soient

PERFECT		PAST SUBJUNCTIVE	
j'	ai été	je	fusse
tu	as été	tu	fusses
il	a été	il	fût
nous	avons été	nous	fussions
vous	avez été	vous	fussiez
ils	ont été	ils	fussent

CONSTRUCTIONS

il est peintre he's a painter

quel jour sommes-nous? – nous sommes le 12 mars
what's today's date? – it's March 12th

à qui est ce cahier? – il est à elle whose jotter is this? –
it's hers

43 faire

to do; to make

also **contrefaire**
to forge

PRESENT PARTICIPLE
faisant

défaire
to undo

PAST PARTICIPLE
fait

refaire
to redo

PRESENT		*IMPERFECT*	
je	fais	je	faisais
tu	fais	tu	faisais
il	fait	il	faisait
nous	faisons	nous	faisions
vous	faites	vous	faisiez
ils	font	ils	faisaient

		FUTURE	
		je	ferai
		tu	feras
		il	fera
		nous	ferons
		vous	ferez
		ils	feront

IMPERATIVE		*CONDITIONAL*	
	fais	je	ferais
	faisons	tu	ferais
	faites	il	ferais
		nous	ferions
		vous	feriez
		ils	feraient

to do; to make

satisfaire
to satisfy

PAST HISTORIC		*PRESENT SUBJUNCTIVE*	
je	fis	je	fasse
tu	fis	tu	fasses
il	fit	il	fasse
nous	fîmes	nous	fassions
vous	fîtes	vous	fassiez
ils	firent	ils	fassent

PERFECT		*PAST SUBJUNCTIVE*	
j'	ai fait	je	fisse
tu	as fait	tu	fisses
il	a fait	il	fît
nous	avons fait	nous	fissions
vous	avez fait	vous	fissiez
ils	ont fait	ils	fissent

CONSTRUCTIONS
faire la vaisselle/la cuisine   to do the dishes/the cooking
faire une promenade/des courses   to go for a walk/go shopping
il fait beau/du vent   it's nice/windy
faire faire qch   to have sth done *or* made

44 falloir
to be necessary

PRESENT PARTICIPLE
not used

PAST PARTICIPLE
fallu

PRESENT	*IMPERFECT*
il faut	**il fallait**
	FUTURE
	il faudra
IMPERATIVE	*CONDITIONAL*
not used	**il faudrait**

PAST HISTORIC **il fallut**	*PRESENT SUBJUNCTIVE* **il faille**
PERFECT **il a fallu**	*PAST SUBJUNCTIVE* **il fallût**

CONSTRUCTIONS

il lui faut quelqu'un pour l'aider he needs somebody to help him

il faut qu'il parte he'll have to *or* has to go

il faut être prudent you have to be careful

45 finir
to finish

also **agir**
to act

PRESENT PARTICIPLE
finissant

bâtir
to build

PAST PARTICIPLE
fini

durcir
to harden

PRESENT

je	finis
tu	finis
il	finit
nous	finissons
vous	finissez
ils	finissent

IMPERATIVE

finis
finissons
finissez

IMPERFECT

je	finissais
tu	finissais
il	finissait
nous	finissions
vous	finissiez
ils	finissaient

FUTURE

je	finirai
tu	finiras
il	finira
nous	finirons
vous	finirez
ils	finiront

CONDITIONAL

je	finirais
tu	finirais
il	finirait
nous	finirions
vous	finiriez
ils	finiraient

guérir
to heal

réunir
to reunite

PAST HISTORIC		PRESENT SUBJUNCTIVE	
je	finis	je	finisse
tu	finis	tu	finisses
il	finit	il	finisse
nous	finîmes	nous	finissions
vous	finîtes	vous	finissiez
ils	finirent	ils	finissent

PERFECT		PAST SUBJUNCTIVE	
j'	ai fini	je	finisse
tu	as fini	tu	finisses
il	a fini	il	finît
nous	avons fini	nous	finissions
vous	avez fini	vous	finissiez
ils	ont fini	ils	finissent

CONSTRUCTIONS

finir de faire qch to finish doing sth
il a fini par comprendre he finally understood
tout finira par s'arranger everything will work out in the end
le film finit bien the film has a happy ending

46 fuir

to flee

also **s'enfuir**

to run away

PRESENT PARTICIPLE
fuyant

PAST PARTICIPLE
fui

PRESENT		*IMPERFECT*	
je	**fuis**	je	**fuyais**
tu	**fuis**	tu	**fuyais**
il	**fuit**	il	**fuyait**
nous	**fuyons**	nous	**fuyions**
vous	**fuyez**	vous	**fuyiez**
ils	**fuient**	ils	**fuyaient**

		FUTURE	
		je	**fuirai**
		tu	**fuiras**
		il	**fuira**
		nous	**fuirons**
		vous	**fuirez**
		ils	**fuiront**

IMPERATIVE		*CONDITIONAL*	
	fuis	je	**fuirais**
	fuyons	tu	**fuirais**
	fuyez	il	**fuirait**
		nous	**fuirions**
		vous	**fuiriez**
		ils	**fuiraient**

PAST HISTORIC		PRESENT SUBJUNCTIVE	
je	fuis	je	fuie
tu	fuis	tu	fuies
il	fuit	il	fuie
nous	fuîmes	nous	fuyions
vous	fuîtes	vous	fuyiez
ils	fuirent	ils	fuient

PERFECT		PAST SUBJUNCTIVE	
j'	ai fui	je	fuisse
tu	as fui	tu	fuisses
il	a fui	il	fuît
nous	avons fui	nous	fuissions
vous	avez fui	vous	fuissiez
ils	ont fui	ils	fuissent

CONSTRUCTIONS
fuir devant un danger/ses responsabilités   to run away
from danger/one's responsibilities

47 haïr

to hate

PRESENT PARTICIPLE
haïssant

PAST PARTICIPLE
haï

PRESENT		*IMPERFECT*	
je	hais	je	haïssais
tu	hais	tu	haïssais
il	hait	il	haïssait
nous	haïssons	nous	haïssions
vous	haïssez	vous	haïssiez
ils	haïssent	ils	haïssaient

		FUTURE	
		je	haïrai
		tu	haïras
		il	haïra
		nous	haïrons
		vous	haïrez
		ils	haïront

IMPERATIVE		*CONDITIONAL*	
	hais	je	haïrais
	haïssons	tu	haïrais
	haïssez	il	haïrait
		nous	haïrions
		vous	haïriez
		ils	haïraient

PAST HISTORIC		PRESENT SUBJUNCTIVE	
je	haïs	je	haïsse
tu	haïs	tu	haïsses
il	haït	il	haïsse
nous	haïmes	nous	haïssions
vous	haïtes	vous	haïssiez
ils	haïrent	ils	haïssent

PERFECT		PAST SUBJUNCTIVE	
j'	ai haï	je	haïsse
tu	as haï	tu	haïsses
il	a haï	il	haït
nous	avons haï	nous	haïssions
vous	avez haï	vous	haïssiez
ils	ont haï	ils	haïssent

48 interdire
to forbid

also **contredire**
to contradict

PRESENT PARTICIPLE
interdisant

prédire
to predict

PAST PARTICIPLE
interdit

PRESENT

j'	interdis
tu	interdis
il	interdit
nous	interdisons
vous	interdisez
ils	interdisent

IMPERFECT

j'	interdisais
tu	interdisais
il	interdisait
nous	interdisions
vous	interdisiez
ils	interdisaient

FUTURE

j'	interdirai
tu	interdiras
il	interdira
nous	interdirons
vous	interdirez
ils	interdiront

IMPERATIVE

interdis
interdisons
interdisez

CONDITIONAL

j'	interdirais
tu	interdirais
il	interdirait
nous	interdirions
vous	interdiriez
ils	interdiraient

to forbid

PAST HISTORIC		PRESENT SUBJUNCTIVE	
j'	interdis	j'	interdise
tu	interdis	tu	interdises
il	interdit	il	interdise
nous	interdîmes	nous	interdisions
vous	interdîtes	vous	interdisiez
ils	interdirent	ils	interdisent

PERFECT		PAST SUBJUNCTIVE	
j'	ai interdit	j'	interdisse
tu	as interdit	tu	interdisses
il	a interdit	il	interdît
nous	avons interdit	nous	interdissions
vous	avez interdit	vous	interdissiez
ils	ont interdit	ils	interdissent

CONSTRUCTIONS

interdire à qn de faire qch   to forbid sb to do sth
il m'a interdit l'alcool/le tabac   he's forbidden me to drink/smoke
il est interdit de fumer   smoking is prohibited
stationnement interdit   no parking

49 introduire
to introduce

PRESENT PARTICIPLE
introduisant

PAST PARTICIPLE
introduit

PRESENT		*IMPERFECT*	
j'	introduis	j'	introduisais
tu	introduis	tu	introduisais
il	introduit	il	introduisait
nous	introduisons	nous	introduisions
vous	introduisez	vous	introduisiez
ils	introduisent	ils	introduisaient
		FUTURE	
		j'	introduirai
		tu	introduiras
		il	introduira
		nous	introduirons
		vous	introduirez
		ils	introduiront
IMPERATIVE		*CONDITIONAL*	
	introduis	j'	introduirais
	introduisons	tu	introduirais
	introduisez	il	introduirait
		nous	introduirions
		vous	introduiriez
		ils	introduiraient

to introduce

PAST HISTORIC		PRESENT SUBJUNCTIVE	
j'	introduisis	j'	introduise
tu	introduisis	tu	introduises
il	introduisit	il	introduise
nous	introduisîmes	nous	introduisions
vous	introduisîtes	vous	introduisiez
ils	introduisirent	ils	introduisent

PERFECT		PAST SUBJUNCTIVE	
j'	ai introduit	j'	introduisisse
tu	as introduit	tu	introduisisses
il	a introduit	il	introduisît
nous	avons introduit	nous	introduisissions
vous	avez introduit	vous	introduisissiez
ils	ont introduit	ils	introduisissent

CONSTRUCTIONS

il a introduit sa clef dans la serrure he inserted his key in the lock

il m'a introduit dans le salon he showed me into the lounge

s'introduire dans une pièce to get into a room

50 jeter
to throw

also **breveter**
to patent

PRESENT PARTICIPLE
jetant

étiqueter
to label

PAST PARTICIPLE
jeté

feuilleter
to leaf through

PRESENT		IMPERFECT	
je	**jette**	je	**jetais**
tu	**jettes**	tu	**jetais**
il	**jette**	il	**jetait**
nous	**jetons**	nous	**jetions**
vous	**jetez**	vous	**jetiez**
ils	**jettent**	ils	**jetaient**

FUTURE
je	**jetterai**
tu	**jetteras**
il	**jettera**
nous	**jetterons**
vous	**jetterez**
ils	**jetteront**

IMPERATIVE
jette
jetons
jetez

CONDITIONAL
je	**jetterais**
tu	**jetterais**
il	**jetterait**
nous	**jetterions**
vous	**jetteriez**
ils	**jetteraient**

projeter
to plan

rejeter
to reject

PAST HISTORIC		PRESENT SUBJUNCTIVE	
je	jetai	je	jette
tu	jetas	tu	jettes
il	jeta	il	jette
nous	jetâmes	nous	jetions
vous	jetâtes	vous	jetiez
ils	jetèrent	ils	jettent

PERFECT		PAST SUBJUNCTIVE	
j'	ai jeté	je	jetasse
tu	as jeté	tu	jetasses
il	a jeté	il	jetât
nous	avons jeté	nous	jetassions
vous	avez jeté	vous	jetassiez
ils	ont jeté	ils	jetassent

CONSTRUCTIONS
jeter qch à qn to throw sth to sb; to throw sth at sb
jeter qch par terre/par la fenêtre to throw sth down/out of the window
jeter qn dehors *or* **à la porte** to throw sb out

51 joindre
to join

also **adjoindre**
to attach

PRESENT PARTICIPLE
joignant

rejoindre
to rejoin

PAST PARTICIPLE
joint

PRESENT	*IMPERFECT*
je **joins**	je **joignais**
tu **joins**	tu **joignais**
il **joint**	il **joignait**
nous **joignons**	nous **joignions**
vous **joignez**	vous **joigniez**
ils **joignent**	ils **joignaient**
	FUTURE
	je **joindrai**
	tu **joindras**
	il **joindra**
	nous **joindrons**
	vous **joindrez**
	ils **joindront**
IMPERATIVE	*CONDITIONAL*
joins	je **joindrais**
joignons	tu **joindrais**
joignez	il **joindrait**
	nous **joindrions**
	vous **joindriez**
	ils **joindraient**

to join

PAST HISTORIC		PRESENT SUBJUNCTIVE	
je	joignis	je	joigne
tu	joignis	tu	joignes
il	joignit	il	joigne
nous	joignîmes	nous	joignions
vous	joignîtes	vous	joigniez
ils	joignirent	ils	joignent

PERFECT		PAST SUBJUNCTIVE	
j'	ai joint	je	joignisse
tu	as joint	tu	joignisses
il	a joint	il	joignît
nous	avons joint	nous	joignissions
vous	avez joint	vous	joignissiez
ils	ont joint	ils	joignissent

CONSTRUCTIONS

joindre les mains to clasp one's hands (together)
voir la lettre ci-jointe see the enclosed letter
elle joint l'intelligence à la beauté she combines
intelligence and beauty
se joindre à to join

52 lever
to lift

also **amener**
to bring

PRESENT PARTICIPLE
levant

élever
to raise

PAST PARTICIPLE
levé

enlever
to remove

PRESENT		*IMPERFECT*	
je	lève	je	levais
tu	lèves	tu	levais
il	lève	il	levait
nous	levons	nous	levions
vous	levez	vous	leviez
ils	lèvent	ils	levaient

		FUTURE	
		je	lèverai
		tu	lèveras
		il	lèvera
		nous	lèverons
		vous	lèverez
		ils	lèveront

IMPERATIVE		*CONDITIONAL*	
	lève	je	lèverais
	levons	tu	lèverais
	levez	il	lèverait
		nous	lèverions
		vous	lèveriez
		ils	lèveraient

mener
to lead

peser
to weigh

PAST HISTORIC		*PRESENT SUBJUNCTIVE*	
je	levai	je	lève
tu	levas	tu	lèves
il	leva	il	lève
nous	levâmes	nous	levions
vous	levâtes	vous	leviez
ils	levèrent	ils	lèvent

PERFECT		*PAST SUBJUNCTIVE*	
j′	ai levé	je	levasse
tu	as levé	tu	levasses
il	a levé	il	levât
nous	avons levé	nous	levassions
vous	avez levé	vous	levassiez
ils	ont levé	ils	levassent

CONSTRUCTIONS
lever les yeux to look up
levez la main! put your hand up!
lever son verre à qn to raise one's glass to sb
se lever to get up; to rise
le jour/la brume se lève day breaks/the mist is clearing

53 lire

to read

also **élire**
to elect

PRESENT PARTICIPLE
lisant

PAST PARTICIPLE
lu

PRESENT		*IMPERFECT*	
je	**lis**	je	**lisais**
tu	**lis**	tu	**lisais**
il	**lit**	il	**lisait**
nous	**lisons**	nous	**lisions**
vous	**lisez**	vous	**lisiez**
ils	**lisent**	ils	**lisaient**

		FUTURE	
		je	**lirai**
		tu	**liras**
		il	**lira**
		nous	**lirons**
		vous	**lirez**
		ils	**liront**

IMPERATIVE	*CONDITIONAL*	
lis	je	**lirais**
lisons	tu	**lirais**
lisez	il	**lirait**
	nous	**lirions**
	vous	**liriez**
	ils	**liraient**

PAST HISTORIC		PRESENT SUBJUNCTIVE	
je	lus	je	lise
tu	lus	tu	lises
il	lut	il	lise
nous	lûmes	nous	lisions
vous	lûtes	vous	lisiez
ils	lurent	ils	lisent
PERFECT		PAST SUBJUNCTIVE	
j'	ai lu	je	lusse
tu	as lu	tu	lusses
il	a lu	il	lût
nous	avons lu	nous	lussions
vous	avez lu	vous	lussiez
ils	ont lu	ils	lussent

CONSTRUCTIONS
je lui ai lu une histoire I read him a story
c'est un livre à lire it's a book you should read

119

54 manger

to eat

also **arranger**
to arrange

PRESENT PARTICIPLE
mangeant

bouger
to move

PAST PARTICIPLE
mangé

dégager
to clear

PRESENT		*IMPERFECT*	
je	mange	je	mangeais
tu	manges	tu	mangeais
il	mange	il	mangeait
nous	mangeons	nous	mangions
vous	mangez	vous	mangiez
ils	mangent	ils	mangeaient

		FUTURE	
		je	mangerai
		tu	mangeras
		il	mangera
		nous	mangerons
		vous	mangerez
		ils	mangeront

IMPERATIVE		*CONDITIONAL*	
	mange	je	mangerais
	mangeons	tu	mangerais
	mangez	il	mangerait
		nous	mangerions
		vous	mangeriez
		ils	mangeraient

diriger
to manage

to eat

loger
to accommodate

PAST HISTORIC		PRESENT SUBJUNCTIVE	
je	mangeai	je	mange
tu	mangeas	tu	manges
il	mangea	il	mange
nous	mangeâmes	nous	mangions
vous	mangeâtes	vous	mangiez
ils	mangèrent	ils	mangent

PERFECT		PAST SUBJUNCTIVE	
j'	ai mangé	je	mangeasse
tu	as mangé	tu	mangeasses
il	a mangé	il	mangeât
nous	avons mangé	nous	mangeassions
vous	avez mangé	vous	mangeassiez
ils	ont mangé	ils	mangeassent

CONSTRUCTIONS
manger comme quatre to eat like a horse
est-ce que ça se mange? is it edible?

55 maudire
to curse

PRESENT PARTICIPLE
maudissant

PAST PARTICIPLE
maudit

PRESENT		*IMPERFECT*	
je	maudis	je	maudissais
tu	maudis	tu	maudissais
il	maudit	il	maudissait
nous	maudissons	nous	maudissions
vous	maudissez	vous	maudissiez
ils	maudissent	ils	maudissaient

		FUTURE	
		je	maudirai
		tu	maudiras
		il	maudira
		nous	maudirons
		vous	maudirez
		ils	maudiront

IMPERATIVE		*CONDITIONAL*	
	maudis	je	maudirais
	maudissons	tu	maudirais
	maudissez	il	maudirait
		nous	maudirions
		vous	maudiriez
		ils	maudiraient

PAST HISTORIC		*PRESENT SUBJUNCTIVE*	
je	maudis	je	maudisse
tu	maudis	tu	maudisses
il	maudit	il	maudisse
nous	maudîmes	nous	maudissions
vous	maudîtes	vous	maudissiez
ils	maudirent	ils	maudissent

PERFECT		*PAST SUBJUNCTIVE*	
j'	ai maudit	je	maudisse
tu	as maudit	tu	maudisses
il	a maudit	il	maudît
nous	avons maudit	nous	maudissions
vous	avez maudit	vous	maudissiez
ils	ont maudit	ils	maudissent

CONSTRUCTIONS

ce maudit stylo ne marche pas!   this blasted pen won't work!

56 mettre
to put

also **admettre**
to admit

PRESENT PARTICIPLE
mettant

commettre
to commit

PAST PARTICIPLE
mis

émettre
to emit

PRESENT

je	mets
tu	mets
il	met
nous	mettons
vous	mettez
ils	mettent

IMPERFECT

je	mettais
tu	mettais
il	mettait
nous	mettions
vous	mettiez
ils	mettaient

FUTURE

je	mettrai
tu	mettras
il	mettra
nous	mettrons
vous	mettrez
ils	mettront

IMPERATIVE

mets
mettons
mettez

CONDITIONAL

je	mettrais
tu	mettrais
il	mettrait
nous	mettrions
vous	mettriez
ils	mettraient

soumettre
to submit

transmettre
to transmit

PAST HISTORIC		PRESENT SUBJUNCTIVE	
je	mis	je	mette
tu	mis	tu	mettes
il	mit	il	mette
nous	mîmes	nous	mettions
vous	mîtes	vous	mettiez
ils	mirent	ils	mettent

PERFECT		PAST SUBJUNCTIVE	
j'	ai mis	je	misse
tu	as mis	tu	misses
il	a mis	il	mît
nous	avons mis	nous	missions
vous	avez mis	vous	missiez
ils	ont mis	ils	missent

CONSTRUCTIONS
j'ai mis 2 heures à le faire   I took 2 hours to do it
elle n'a rien à se mettre   she's nothing to wear
se mettre à faire qch   to start doing sth
se mettre au travail   to set to work

57 monter

to go up

PRESENT PARTICIPLE
montant

PAST PARTICIPLE
monté

PRESENT		*IMPERFECT*	
je	monte	je	montais
tu	montes	tu	montais
il	monte	il	montait
nous	montons	nous	montions
vous	montez	vous	montiez
ils	montent	ils	montaient

		FUTURE	
		je	monterai
		tu	monteras
		il	montera
		nous	monterons
		vous	monterez
		ils	monteront

IMPERATIVE		*CONDITIONAL*	
	monte	je	monterais
	montons	tu	monterais
	montez	il	monterait
		nous	monterions
		vous	monteriez
		ils	monteraient

to go up

PAST HISTORIC		PRESENT SUBJUNCTIVE	
je	montai	je	monte
tu	montas	tu	montes
il	monta	il	monte
nous	montâmes	nous	montions
vous	montâtes	vous	montiez
ils	montèrent	ils	montent

PERFECT		PAST SUBJUNCTIVE	
je	suis monté	je	montasse
tu	es monté	tu	montasses
il	est monté	il	montât
nous	sommes montés	nous	montassions
vous	êtes monté(s)	vous	montassiez
ils	sont montés	ils	montassent

CONSTRUCTIONS

monter dans un train/un avion   to get on a train/plane
monter en voiture   to get into a car
monter à bicyclette/cheval   to get on a bicycle/horse; to ride a bicycle/horse
il a monté la valise   he took the case up

58 mordre
to bite

also **tordre**
to twist

PRESENT PARTICIPLE
mordant

PAST PARTICIPLE
mordu

PRESENT		*IMPERFECT*	
je	mords	je	mordais
tu	mords	tu	mordais
il	mord	il	mordait
nous	mordons	nous	mordions
vous	mordez	vous	mordiez
ils	mordent	ils	mordaient

		FUTURE	
		je	mordrai
		tu	mordras
		il	mordra
		nous	mordrons
		vous	mordrez
		ils	mordront

IMPERATIVE		*CONDITIONAL*	
	mords	je	mordrais
	mordons	tu	mordrais
	mordez	il	mordrait
		nous	mordrions
		vous	mordriez
		ils	mordraient

PAST HISTORIC		PRESENT SUBJUNCTIVE	
je	mordis	je	morde
tu	mordis	tu	mordes
il	mordit	il	morde
nous	mordîmes	nous	mordions
vous	mordîtes	vous	mordiez
ils	mordirent	ils	mordent

PERFECT		PAST SUBJUNCTIVE	
j'	ai mordu	je	mordisse
tu	as mordu	tu	mordisses
il	a mordu	il	mordît
nous	avons mordu	nous	mordissions
vous	avez mordu	vous	mordissiez
ils	ont mordu	ils	mordissent

CONSTRUCTIONS

mordre qn à la main to bite sb's hand
mordre dans une pomme to bite into an apple
mordu de football mad keen on football
mordre à l'hameçon to rise to the bait

59 moudre
to grind

PRESENT PARTICIPLE
moulant

PAST PARTICIPLE
moulu

PRESENT

je	**mouds**
tu	**mouds**
il	**moud**
nous	**moulons**
vous	**moulez**
ils	**moulent**

IMPERFECT

je	**moulais**
tu	**moulais**
il	**moulait**
nous	**moulions**
vous	**mouliez**
ils	**moulaient**

FUTURE

je	**moudrai**
tu	**moudras**
il	**moudra**
nous	**moudrons**
vous	**moudrez**
ils	**moudront**

IMPERATIVE

mouds
moulons
moulez

CONDITIONAL

je	**moudrais**
tu	**moudrais**
il	**moudrait**
nous	**moudrions**
vous	**moudriez**
ils	**moudraient**

moudre 59
to grind

PAST HISTORIC		PRESENT SUBJUNCTIVE	
je	moulus	je	moule
tu	moulus	tu	moules
il	moulut	il	moule
nous	moulûmes	nous	moulions
vous	moulûtes	vous	mouliez
ils	moulurent	ils	moulent

PERFECT		PAST SUBJUNCTIVE	
j'	ai moulu	je	moulusse
tu	as moulu	tu	moulusses
il	a moulu	il	moulût
nous	avons moulu	nous	moulussions
vous	avez moulu	vous	moulussiez
ils	ont moulu	ils	moulussent

CONSTRUCTIONS
je l'aimerais moulu très fin, s'il vous plaît   I'd like it very finely ground, please

60 mourir
to die

PRESENT PARTICIPLE
mourant

PAST PARTICIPLE
mort

PRESENT		*IMPERFECT*	
je	**meurs**	je	**mourais**
tu	**meurs**	tu	**mourais**
il	**meurt**	il	**mourait**
nous	**mourons**	nous	**mourions**
vous	**mourez**	vous	**mouriez**
ils	**meurent**	ils	**mouraient**

		FUTURE	
		je	**mourrai**
		tu	**mourras**
		il	**mourra**
		nous	**mourrons**
		vous	**mourrez**
		ils	**mourront**

IMPERATIVE		*CONDITIONAL*	
	meurs	je	**mourrais**
	mourons	tu	**mourrais**
	mourez	il	**mourrait**
		nous	**mourrions**
		vous	**mourriez**
		ils	**mourraient**

PAST HISTORIC		PRESENT SUBJUNCTIVE	
je	mourus	je	meure
tu	mourus	tu	meures
il	mourut	il	meure
nous	mourûmes	nous	mourions
vous	mourûtes	vous	mouriez
ils	moururent	ils	meurent

PERFECT		PAST SUBJUNCTIVE	
je	suis mort	je	mourusse
tu	es mort	tu	mourusses
il	est mort	il	mourût
nous	sommes mort	nous	mourussions
vous	êtes mort(s)	vous	mourussiez
ils	sont morts	ils	mourussent

CONSTRUCTIONS
il est mort he's dead
il est mort en 1960 he died in 1960
mourir de faim/froid to die of hunger/cold
être mort de peur to be scared to death
mourir d'envie de faire qch to be dying to do sth

61 mouvoir
to move

PRESENT PARTICIPLE
mouvant

PAST PARTICIPLE
mû (*NB*: **mue, mus, mues**)

PRESENT		*IMPERFECT*	
je	**meus**	je	**mouvais**
tu	**meus**	tu	**mouvais**
il	**meut**	il	**mouvait**
nous	**mouvons**	nous	**mouvions**
vous	**mouvez**	vous	**mouviez**
ils	**meuvent**	ils	**mouvaient**

		FUTURE	
		je	**mouvrai**
		tu	**mouvras**
		il	**mouvra**
		nous	**mouvrons**
		vous	**mouvrez**
		ils	**mouvront**

IMPERATIVE	*CONDITIONAL*	
meus	je	**mouvrais**
mouvons	tu	**mouvrais**
mouvez	il	**mouvrait**
	nous	**mouvrions**
	vous	**mouvriez**
	ils	**mouvraient**

to move

PAST HISTORIC		PRESENT SUBJUNCTIVE	
je	mus	je	meuve
tu	mus	tu	meuves
il	mut	il	meuve
nous	mûmes	nous	mouvions
vous	mûtes	vous	mouviez
ils	murent	ils	meuvent

PERFECT		PAST SUBJUNCTIVE	
j'	ai mû	je	musse
tu	as mû	tu	musses
il	a mû	il	mût
nous	avons mû	nous	mussions
vous	avez mû	vous	mussiez
ils	ont mû	ils	mussent

CONSTRUCTIONS
il a de la peine à se mouvoir   he has difficulty in moving

62 naître
to be born

PRESENT PARTICIPLE
naissant

PAST PARTICIPLE
né

	PRESENT		*IMPERFECT*
je	nais	je	naissais
tu	nais	tu	naissais
il	naît	il	naissait
nous	naissons	nous	naissions
vous	naissez	vous	naissiez
ils	naissent	ils	naissaient

	FUTURE
je	naîtrai
tu	naîtras
il	naîtra
nous	naîtrons
vous	naîtrez
ils	naîtront

	IMPERATIVE		*CONDITIONAL*
	nais	je	naîtrais
	naissons	tu	naîtrais
	naissez	il	naîtrait
		nous	naîtrions
		vous	naîtriez
		ils	naîtraient

PAST HISTORIC		PRESENT SUBJUNCTIVE	
je	naquis	je	naisse
tu	naquis	tu	naisses
il	naquit	il	naisse
nous	naquîmes	nous	naissions
vous	naquîtes	vous	naissiez
ils	naquirent	ils	naissent

PERFECT		PAST SUBJUNCTIVE	
je	suis né	je	naquisse
tu	es né	tu	naquisses
il	est né	il	naquît
nous	sommes nés	nous	naquissions
vous	êtes né(s)	vous	naquissiez
ils	sont nés	ils	naquissent

CONSTRUCTIONS

je suis né le 5 mars I was born on 5th March

il naît plus de filles que de garçons there are more girls born than boys

faire naître des soupçons to arouse suspicion

63 nettoyer
to clean

also **aboyer**
to bark

PRESENT PARTICIPLE
nettoyant

appuyer
to lean

PAST PARTICIPLE
nettoyé

employer
to use

PRESENT		*IMPERFECT*	
je	nettoie	je	nettoyais
tu	nettoies	tu	nettoyais
il	nettoie	il	nettoyait
nous	nettoyons	nous	nettoyions
vous	nettoyez	vous	nettoyiez
ils	nettoient	ils	nettoyaient

		FUTURE	
		je	nettoierai
		tu	nettoieras
		il	nettoiera
		nous	nettoierons
		vous	nettoierez
		ils	nettoieront

IMPERATIVE		*CONDITIONAL*	
	nettoie	je	nettoierais
	nettoyons	tu	nettoierais
	nettoyez	il	nettoierait
		nous	nettoierions
		vous	nettoieriez
		ils	nettoieraient

ennuyer
to bore

essuyer
to wipe

PAST HISTORIC		*PRESENT SUBJUNCTIVE*	
je	nettoyai	je	nettoie
tu	nettoyas	tu	nettoies
il	nettoya	il	nettoie
nous	nettoyâmes	nous	nettoyions
vous	nettoyâtes	vous	nettoyiez
ils	nettoyèrent	ils	nettoient

PERFECT		*PAST SUBJUNCTIVE*	
j'	ai nettoyé	je	nettoyasse
tu	as nettoyé	tu	nettoyasses
il	a nettoyé	il	nettoyât
nous	avons nettoyé	nous	nettoyassions
vous	avez nettoyé	vous	nettoyassiez
ils	ont nettoyé	ils	nettoyassent

CONSTRUCTIONS
nettoyer à sec to dry-clean

64 obtenir
to get

PRESENT PARTICIPLE
obtenant

PAST PARTICIPLE
obtenu

PRESENT		IMPERFECT	
j'	**obtiens**	j'	**obtenais**
tu	**obtiens**	tu	**obtenais**
il	**obtient**	il	**obtenait**
nous	**obtenons**	nous	**obtenions**
vous	**obtenez**	vous	**obteniez**
ils	**obtiennent**	ils	**obtenaient**

FUTURE	
j'	**obtiendrai**
tu	**obtiendras**
il	**obtiendra**
nous	**obtiendrons**
vous	**obtiendrez**
ils	**obtiendront**

IMPERATIVE	CONDITIONAL	
obtiens	j'	**obtiendrais**
obtenons	tu	**obtiendrais**
obtenez	il	**obtiendrait**
	nous	**obtiendrions**
	vous	**obtiendriez**
	ils	**obtiendraient**

obtenir 64
to get

PAST HISTORIC		PRESENT SUBJUNCTIVE	
j'	obtins	j'	obtienne
tu	obtins	tu	obtiennes
il	obtint	il	obtienne
nous	obtînmes	nous	obtenions
vous	obtîntes	vous	obteniez
ils	obtinrent	ils	obtiennent

PERFECT		PAST SUBJUNCTIVE	
j'	ai obtenu	j'	obtinsse
tu	as obtenu	tu	obtinsses
il	a obtenu	il	obtînt
nous	avons obtenu	nous	obtinssions
vous	avez obtenu	vous	obtinssiez
ils	ont obtenu	ils	obtinssent

CONSTRUCTIONS

obtenir qch de qn   to get sth from sb
obtenir de qn qu'il fasse qch   to get sb to do sth

65 offrir
to offer

also **souffrir**
to suffer

PRESENT PARTICIPLE
offrant

PAST PARTICIPLE
offert

PRESENT		IMPERFECT	
j'	offre	j'	offrais
tu	offres	tu	offrais
il	offre	il	offrait
nous	offrons	nous	offrions
vous	offrez	vous	offriez
ils	offrent	ils	offraient

		FUTURE	
		j'	offrirai
		tu	offriras
		il	offrira
		nous	offrirons
		vous	offrirez
		ils	offriront

IMPERATIVE		CONDITIONAL	
	offre	j'	offrirais
	offrons	tu	offrirais
	offrez	il	offrirait
		nous	offririons
		vous	offririez
		ils	offriraient

PAST HISTORIC		PRESENT SUBJUNCTIVE	
j'	offris	j'	offre
tu	offris	tu	offres
il	offrit	il	offre
nous	offrîmes	nous	offrions
vous	offrîtes	vous	offriez
ils	offrirent	ils	offrent

PERFECT		PAST SUBJUNCTIVE	
j'	ai offert	j'	offrisse
tu	as offert	tu	offrisses
il	a offert	il	offrît
nous	avons offert	nous	offrissions
vous	avez offert	vous	offrissiez
ils	ont offert	ils	offrissent

CONSTRUCTIONS

offrir qch à qn to give sb sth; to offer sb sth
offrir de faire qch to offer to do sth
s'offrir un bon repas/un disque to treat oneself to a good meal/a record
il s'est offert en otage/comme guide he volunteered to be *or* as a hostage/guide

66 ouvrir

to open   *also* **rouvrir**
         to reopen

PRESENT PARTICIPLE
ouvrant

PAST PARTICIPLE
ouvert

PRESENT		*IMPERFECT*	
j'	ouvre	j'	ouvrais
tu	ouvres	tu	ouvrais
il	ouvre	il	ouvrait
nous	ouvrons	nous	ouvrions
vous	ouvrez	vous	ouvriez
ils	ouvrent	ils	ouvraient

		FUTURE	
		j'	ouvrirai
		tu	ouvriras
		il	ouvrira
		nous	ouvrirons
		vous	ouvrirez
		ils	ouvriront

IMPERATIVE		*CONDITIONAL*	
ouvre		j'	ouvrirais
ouvrons		tu	ouvrirais
ouvrez		il	ouvrirait
		nous	ouvririons
		vous	ouvririez
		ils	ouvriraient

PAST HISTORIC		PRESENT SUBJUNCTIVE	
j'	ouvris	j'	ouvre
tu	ouvris	tu	ouvres
il	ouvrit	il	ouvre
nous	ouvrîmes	nous	ouvrions
vous	ouvrîtes	vous	ouvriez
ils	ouvrirent	ils	ouvrent

PERFECT		PAST SUBJUNCTIVE	
j'	ai ouvert	j'	ouvrisse
tu	as ouvert	tu	ouvrisses
il	a ouvert	il	ouvrît
nous	avons ouvert	nous	ouvrissions
vous	avez ouvert	vous	ouvrissiez
ils	ont ouvert	ils	ouvrissent

CONSTRUCTIONS

ouvrir une porte toute grande   to open a door wide
ouvrir l'électricité/le gaz/la radio   to switch *or* turn on
the electricity/gas/radio
notre épicier ouvre le lundi   our grocer is open on
Mondays
s'ouvrir   to open; to open up; to open out

67 paraître

to appear   *also* **disparaître**
to disappear

PRESENT PARTICIPLE
paraissant

PAST PARTICIPLE
paru

PRESENT		*IMPERFECT*	
je	parais	je	paraissais
tu	parais	tu	paraissais
il	paraît	il	paraissait
nous	paraissons	nous	paraissions
vous	paraissez	vous	paraissiez
ils	paraissent	ils	paraissaient

		FUTURE	
		je	paraîtrai
		tu	paraîtras
		il	paraîtra
		nous	paraîtrons
		vous	paraîtrez
		ils	paraîtront

IMPERATIVE	*CONDITIONAL*	
parais	je	paraîtrais
paraissons	tu	paraîtrais
paraissez	il	paraîtrait
	nous	paraîtrions
	vous	paraîtriez
	ils	paraîtraient

PAST HISTORIC		PRESENT SUBJUNCTIVE	
je	parus	je	paraisse
tu	parus	tu	paraisses
il	parut	il	paraisse
nous	parûmes	nous	paraissions
vous	parûtes	vous	paraissiez
ils	parurent	ils	paraissent

PERFECT		PAST SUBJUNCTIVE	
j'	ai paru	je	parusse
tu	as paru	tu	parusses
il	a paru	il	parût
nous	avons paru	nous	parussions
vous	avez paru	vous	parussiez
ils	ont paru	ils	parussent

CONSTRUCTIONS

paraître faire qch to seem to do sth
'vient de paraître' 'just out'
'à paraître prochainement' 'out soon'
il est malade, paraît-il, il paraît qu'il est malade he's ill
apparently

68 partir

to go, leave

PRESENT PARTICIPLE
partant

PAST PARTICIPLE
parti

PRESENT		*IMPERFECT*	
je	**pars**	je	**partais**
tu	**pars**	tu	**partais**
il	**part**	il	**partait**
nous	**partons**	nous	**partions**
vous	**partez**	vous	**partiez**
ils	**partent**	ils	**partaient**

		FUTURE	
		je	**partirai**
		tu	**partiras**
		il	**partira**
		nous	**partirons**
		vous	**partirez**
		ils	**partiront**

IMPERATIVE		*CONDITIONAL*	
	pars	je	**partirais**
	partons	tu	**partirais**
	partez	il	**partirait**
		nous	**partirions**
		vous	**partiriez**
		ils	**partiraient**

partir **68**
to go, leave

PAST HISTORIC		PRESENT SUBJUNCTIVE	
je	partis	je	parte
tu	partis	tu	partes
il	partit	il	parte
nous	partîmes	nous	partions
vous	partîtes	vous	partiez
ils	partirent	ils	partent

PERFECT		PAST SUBJUNCTIVE	
je	suis parti	je	partisse
tu	es parti	tu	partisses
il	est parti	il	partît
nous	sommes partis	nous	partissions
vous	êtes parti(s)	vous	partissiez
ils	sont partis	ils	partissent

CONSTRUCTIONS

partir en vacances/en voyage   to go (off) on holiday/on
a journey
à partir du 14 juillet   as from the 14th of July
à partir de 100 F   from 100 F upwards

69 passer

to pass

also **dépasser**
to overtake

PRESENT PARTICIPLE
passant

surpasser
to surpass

PAST PARTICIPLE
passé

PRESENT		IMPERFECT	
je	passe	je	passais
tu	passes	tu	passais
il	passe	il	passait
nous	passons	nous	passions
vous	passez	vous	passiez
ils	passent	ils	passaient

FUTURE	
je	passerai
tu	passeras
il	passera
nous	passerons
vous	passerez
ils	passeront

IMPERATIVE	CONDITIONAL	
passe	je	passerais
passons	tu	passerais
passez	il	passerait
	nous	passerions
	vous	passeriez
	ils	passeraient

PAST HISTORIC		PRESENT SUBJUNCTIVE	
je	passai	je	passe
tu	passas	tu	passes
il	passa	il	passe
nous	passâmes	nous	passions
vous	passâtes	vous	passiez
ils	passèrent	ils	passent

PERFECT		PAST SUBJUNCTIVE	
j'	ai passé	je	passasse
tu	as passé	tu	passasses
il	a passé	il	passât
nous	avons passé	nous	passassions
vous	avez passé	vous	passassiez
ils	ont passé	ils	passassent

CONSTRUCTIONS

passer en courant to run past
passer au bureau/chez un ami to call (in) at the office/at a friend's
laisser passer qn to let sb through *or* in *etc*
laisser passer une erreur to overlook a mistake
passer un examen to sit an exam

70 payer

to pay

also balayer
to sweep up

PRESENT PARTICIPLE
payant

débrayer
to declutch

PAST PARTICIPLE
payé

délayer
to thin down

PRESENT		IMPERFECT	
je	paye	je	payais
tu	payes	tu	payais
il	paye	il	payait
nous	payons	nous	payions
vous	payez	vous	payiez
ils	payent	ils	payaient

FUTURE	
je	payerai
tu	payeras
il	payera
nous	payerons
vous	payerez
ils	payeront

IMPERATIVE		CONDITIONAL	
	paye	je	payerais
	payons	tu	payerais
	payez	il	payerait
		nous	payerions
		vous	payeriez
		ils	payeraient

effrayer
to frighten

essayer
to try

PAST HISTORIC		PRESENT SUBJUNCTIVE	
je	payai	je	paye
tu	payas	tu	payes
il	paya	il	paye
nous	payâmes	nous	payions
vous	payâtes	vous	payiez
ils	payèrent	ils	payent

PERFECT		PAST SUBJUNCTIVE	
j'	ai payé	je	payasse
tu	as payé	tu	payasses
il	a payé	il	payât
nous	avons payé	nous	payassions
vous	avez payé	vous	payassiez
ils	ont payé	ils	payassent

CONSTRUCTIONS
être payé par chèque/à l'heure to be paid by cheque/by the hour
est-ce qu'il t'a payé les billets? did he pay you for the tickets?
il l'a payé 10 F he paid 10 F for it
il l'a payé de sa vie it cost him his life

71 peindre
to paint

also **atteindre**
to reach

PRESENT PARTICIPLE
peignant

déteindre
to lose its colour

PAST PARTICIPLE
peint

enfreindre
to infringe

PRESENT		IMPERFECT	
je	peins	je	peignais
tu	peins	tu	peignais
il	peint	il	peignait
nous	peignons	nous	peignions
vous	peignez	vous	peigniez
ils	peignent	ils	peignaient

		FUTURE	
		je	peindrai
		tu	peindras
		il	peindra
		nous	peindrons
		vous	peindrez
		ils	peindront

IMPERATIVE		CONDITIONAL	
	peins	je	peindrais
	peignons	tu	peindrais
	peignez	il	peindrait
		nous	peindrions
		vous	peindriez
		ils	peindraient

to paint

éteindre
to put out

teindre
to dye

PAST HISTORIC		PRESENT SUBJUNCTIVE	
je	peignis	je	peigne
tu	peignis	tu	peignes
il	peignit	il	peigne
nous	peignîmes	nous	peignions
vous	peignîtes	vous	peigniez
ils	peignirent	ils	peignent

PERFECT		PAST SUBJUNCTIVE	
j'	ai peint	je	peignisse
tu	as peint	tu	peignisses
il	a peint	il	peignît
nous	avons peint	nous	peignissions
vous	avez peint	vous	peignissiez
ils	ont peint	ils	peignissent

CONSTRUCTIONS
peindre qch en bleu / à l'huile   to paint sth blue / in oils

72 perdre
to lose

PRESENT PARTICIPLE
perdant

PAST PARTICIPLE
perdu

PRESENT			*IMPERFECT*	
je	**perds**		je	**perdais**
tu	**perds**		tu	**perdais**
il	**perd**		il	**perdait**
nous	**perdons**		nous	**perdions**
vous	**perdez**		vous	**perdiez**
ils	**perdent**		ils	**perdaient**
			FUTURE	
			je	**perdrai**
			tu	**perdras**
			il	**perdra**
			nous	**perdrons**
			vous	**perdrez**
			ils	**perdront**
IMPERATIVE			*CONDITIONAL*	
	perds		je	**perdrais**
	perdons		tu	**perdrais**
	perdez		il	**perdrait**
			nous	**perdrions**
			vous	**perdriez**
			ils	**perdraient**

PAST HISTORIC		PRESENT SUBJUNCTIVE	
je	perdis	je	perde
tu	perdis	tu	perdes
il	perdit	il	perde
nous	perdîmes	nous	perdions
vous	perdîtes	vous	perdiez
ils	perdirent	ils	perdent

PERFECT		PAST SUBJUNCTIVE	
j'	ai perdu	je	perdisse
tu	as perdu	tu	perdisses
il	a perdu	il	perdît
nous	avons perdu	nous	perdissions
vous	avez perdu	vous	perdissiez
ils	ont perdu	ils	perdissent

CONSTRUCTIONS

perdre qn/qch de vue to lose sight of sb/sth
perdre espoir/connaissance/du poids to lose
hope/consciousness/weight
tu perds ton temps à essayer you're wasting your time
trying
se perdre to get lost; to disappear

73 permettre
to allow

PRESENT PARTICIPLE
permettant

PAST PARTICIPLE
permis

PRESENT		*IMPERFECT*	
je	**permets**	je	**permettais**
tu	**permets**	tu	**permettais**
il	**permet**	il	**permettait**
nous	**permettons**	nous	**permettions**
vous	**permettez**	vous	**permettiez**
ils	**permettent**	ils	**permettaient**

		FUTURE	
		je	**permettrai**
		tu	**permettras**
		il	**permettra**
		nous	**permettrons**
		vous	**permettrez**
		ils	**permettront**

IMPERATIVE		*CONDITIONAL*	
	permets	je	**permettrais**
	permettons	tu	**permettrais**
	permettez	il	**permettrait**
		nous	**permettrions**
		vous	**permettriez**
		ils	**permettraient**

to allow

PAST HISTORIC		PRESENT SUBJUNCTIVE	
je	permis	je	permette
tu	permis	tu	permettes
il	permit	il	permette
nous	permîmes	nous	permettions
vous	permîtes	vous	permettiez
ils	permirent	ils	permettent

PERFECT		PAST SUBJUNCTIVE	
j'	ai permis	je	permisse
tu	as permis	tu	permisses
il	a permis	il	permît
nous	avons permis	nous	permissions
vous	avez permis	vous	permissiez
ils	ont permis	ils	permissent

CONSTRUCTIONS

permettre à qn de faire qch to allow sb to do sth
permettre qch à qn to allow sb sth
mes moyens ne me le permettent pas I can't afford it
permettez-moi de vous présenter ma sœur may I
introduce my sister?

74 plaire
to please

also **déplaire**
to displease

PRESENT PARTICIPLE
plaisant

PAST PARTICIPLE
plu

PRESENT		IMPERFECT	
je	plais	je	plaisais
tu	plais	tu	plaisais
il	plaît	il	plaisait
nous	plaisons	nous	plaisions
vous	plaisez	vous	plaisiez
ils	plaisent	ils	plaisaient

		FUTURE	
		je	plairai
		tu	plairas
		il	plaira
		nous	plairons
		vous	plairez
		ils	plairont

IMPERATIVE		CONDITIONAL	
plais		je	plairais
plaisons		tu	plairais
plaisez		il	plairait
		nous	plairions
		vous	plairiez
		ils	plairaient

PAST HISTORIC		PRESENT SUBJUNCTIVE	
je	plus	je	plaise
tu	plus	tu	plaises
il	plut	il	plaise
nous	plûmes	nous	plaisions
vous	plûtes	vous	plaisiez
ils	plurent	ils	plaisent

PERFECT		PAST SUBJUNCTIVE	
j'	ai plu	je	plusse
tu	as plu	tu	plusses
il	a plu	il	plût
nous	avons plu	nous	plussions
vous	avez plu	vous	plussiez
ils	ont plu	ils	plussent

CONSTRUCTIONS

sa maison lui plaît   she likes her house
il cherche à plaire à tout le monde   he tries to please everybody
j'irai si ça me plaît   I'll go if I feel like it
s'il te plaît, s'il vous plaît   please
il se plaît à Paris   he likes being in Paris

75 pleuvoir
to rain

PRESENT PARTICIPLE
pleuvant

PAST PARTICIPLE
plu

PRESENT	IMPERFECT
il **pleut**	il **pleuvait**

	FUTURE
	il **pleuvra**

IMPERATIVE	CONDITIONAL
not used	il **pleuvrait**

PAST HISTORIC
il plut

PRESENT SUBJUNCTIVE
il pleuve

PERFECT
il a plu

PAST SUBJUNCTIVE
il plût

CONSTRUCTIONS
il pleut it's raining
il pleut à verse it's pouring

76 pourvoir
to provide

PRESENT PARTICIPLE
pourvoyant

PAST PARTICIPLE
pourvu

PRESENT		*IMPERFECT*	
je	**pourvois**	je	**pourvoyais**
tu	**pourvois**	tu	**pourvoyais**
il	**pourvoit**	il	**pourvoyait**
nous	**pourvoyons**	nous	**pourvoyions**
vous	**pourvoyez**	vous	**pourvoyiez**
ils	**pourvoient**	ils	**pourvoyaient**

		FUTURE	
		je	**pourvoirai**
		tu	**pourvoiras**
		il	**pourvoira**
		nous	**pourvoirons**
		vous	**pourvoirez**
		ils	**pourvoiront**

IMPERATIVE	*CONDITIONAL*	
pourvois	je	**pourvoirais**
pourvoyons	tu	**pourvoirais**
pourvoyez	il	**pourvoirait**
	nous	**pourvoirions**
	vous	**pourvoiriez**
	ils	**pourvoiraient**

PAST HISTORIC		PRESENT SUBJUNCTIVE	
je	pourvus	je	pourvoie
tu	pourvus	tu	pourvoies
il	pourvut	il	pourvoie
nous	pourvûmes	nous	pourvoyions
vous	pourvûtes	vous	pourvoyiez
ils	pourvurent	ils	pourvoient

PERFECT		PAST SUBJUNCTIVE	
j'	ai pourvu	je	pourvusse
tu	as pourvu	tu	pourvusses
il	a pourvu	il	pourvût
nous	avons pourvu	nous	pourvussions
vous	avez pourvu	vous	pourvussiez
ils	ont pourvu	ils	pourvussent

CONSTRUCTIONS

pourvoir qch de qch   to equip sth with sth
pourvoir aux besoins de qn   to provide for sb's needs

77 pouvoir
to be able

PRESENT PARTICIPLE
pouvant

PAST PARTICIPLE
pu

PRESENT		*IMPERFECT*	
je	**peux**	je	**pouvais**
tu	**peux**	tu	**pouvais**
il	**peut**	il	**pouvait**
nous	**pouvons**	nous	**pouvions**
vous	**pouvez**	vous	**pouviez**
ils	**peuvent**	ils	**pouvaient**

		FUTURE	
		je	**pourrai**
		tu	**pourras**
		il	**pourra**
		nous	**pourrons**
		vous	**pourrez**
		ils	**pourront**

IMPERATIVE		*CONDITIONAL*	
	not used	je	**pourrais**
		tu	**pourrais**
		il	**pourrait**
		nous	**pourrions**
		vous	**pourriez**
		ils	**pourraient**

to be able

PAST HISTORIC		PRESENT SUBJUNCTIVE	
je	pus	je	puisse
tu	pus	tu	puisses
il	put	il	puisse
nous	pûmes	nous	puissions
vous	pûtes	vous	puissiez
ils	purent	ils	puissent

PERFECT		PAST SUBJUNCTIVE	
j'	ai pu	je	pusse
tu	as pu	tu	pusses
il	a pu	il	pût
nous	avons pu	nous	pussions
vous	avez pu	vous	pussiez
ils	ont pu	ils	pussent

CONSTRUCTIONS

pouvoir faire to be able to do
il ne peut pas venir he can't come
il n'en peut plus he's tired out; he's had enough
il a été on ne peut plus aimable he couldn't have been kinder

78 prendre
to take

PRESENT PARTICIPLE
prenant

PAST PARTICIPLE
pris

also **entreprendre**
to undertake

se méprendre
to be mistaken

surprendre
to surprise

PRESENT		IMPERFECT	
je	prends	je	prenais
tu	prends	tu	prenais
il	prend	il	prenait
nous	prenons	nous	prenions
vous	prenez	vous	preniez
ils	prennent	ils	prenaient

		FUTURE	
		je	prendrai
		tu	prendras
		il	prendra
		nous	prendrons
		vous	prendrez
		ils	prendront

IMPERATIVE		CONDITIONAL	
	prends	je	prendrais
	prenons	tu	prendrais
	prenez	il	prendrait
		nous	prendrions
		vous	prendriez
		ils	prendraient

PAST HISTORIC		PRESENT SUBJUNCTIVE	
je	pris	je	prenne
tu	pris	tu	prennes
il	prit	il	prenne
nous	prîmes	nous	prenions
vous	prîtes	vous	preniez
ils	prirent	ils	prennent

PERFECT		PAST SUBJUNCTIVE	
j'	ai pris	je	prisse
tu	as pris	tu	prisses
il	a pris	il	prît
nous	avons pris	nous	prissions
vous	avez pris	vous	prissiez
ils	ont pris	ils	prissent

CONSTRUCTIONS

prendre qch à qn to take sth from sb
il l'a pris dans un tiroir/sur la table he took it out of a drawer/from the table
prendre feu to catch fire
prendre qn en amitié/en aversion to take a liking/a dislike to sb

79 promettre
to promise

also **compromettre**
to compromise

PRESENT PARTICIPLE
promettant

PAST PARTICIPLE
promis

PRESENT		IMPERFECT	
je	promets	je	promettais
tu	promets	tu	promettais
il	promet	il	promettait
nous	promettons	nous	promettions
vous	promettez	vous	promettiez
ils	promettent	ils	promettaient

		FUTURE	
		je	promettrai
		tu	promettras
		il	promettra
		nous	promettrons
		vous	promettrez
		ils	promettront

IMPERATIVE	CONDITIONAL	
promets	je	promettrais
promettons	tu	promettrais
promettez	il	promettrait
	nous	promettrions
	vous	promettriez
	ils	promettraient

to promise

PAST HISTORIC		PRESENT SUBJUNCTIVE	
je	promis	je	promette
tu	promis	tu	promettes
il	promit	il	promette
nous	promîmes	nous	promettions
vous	promîtes	vous	promettiez
ils	promirent	ils	promettent

PERFECT		PAST SUBJUNCTIVE	
j'	ai promis	je	promisse
tu	as promis	tu	promisses
il	a promis	il	promît
nous	avons promis	nous	promissions
vous	avez promis	vous	promissiez
ils	ont promis	ils	promissent

CONSTRUCTIONS

promettre qch à qn to promise sth to sb
promettre à qn de faire qch to promise sb that one will do sth
on nous promet du beau temps we're in for some fine weather, they say
se promettre de faire to resolve to do

171

80 protéger

to protect

also **abréger**
to shorten

PRESENT PARTICIPLE
protégeant

alléger
to lighten

PAST PARTICIPLE
protégé

assiéger
to besiege

PRESENT		*IMPERFECT*	
je	protège	je	protégeais
tu	protèges	tu	protégeais
il	protège	il	protégeait
nous	protégeons	nous	protégions
vous	protégez	vous	protégiez
ils	protègent	ils	protégeaient

		FUTURE	
		je	protégerai
		tu	protégeras
		il	protégera
		nous	protégerons
		vous	protégerez
		ils	protégeront

IMPERATIVE	*CONDITIONAL*	
protège	je	protégerais
protégeons	tu	protégerais
protégez	il	protégerait
	nous	protégerions
	vous	protégeriez
	ils	protégeraient

piéger
to booby-trap

PAST HISTORIC		PRESENT SUBJUNCTIVE	
je	protégeai	je	protège
tu	protégeas	tu	protèges
il	protégea	il	protège
nous	protégeâmes	nous	protégions
vous	protégeâtes	vous	protégiez
ils	protégèrent	ils	protègent

PERFECT		PAST SUBJUNCTIVE	
j'	ai protégé	je	protégeasse
tu	as protégé	tu	protégeasses
il	a protégé	il	protégeât
nous	avons protégé	nous	protégeassions
vous	avez protégé	vous	protégeassiez
ils	ont protégé	ils	protégeassent

CONSTRUCTIONS
se protéger de qch / contre qch   to protect oneself from
sth / against sth

81 recevoir
to receive

also **apercevoir**
to see

PRESENT PARTICIPLE
recevant

décevoir
to disappoint

PAST PARTICIPLE
reçu

percevoir
to perceive

PRESENT		*IMPERFECT*	
je	reçois	je	recevais
tu	reçois	tu	recevais
il	reçoit	il	recevait
nous	recevons	nous	recevions
vous	recevez	vous	receviez
ils	reçoivent	ils	recevaient

FUTURE	
je	recevrai
tu	recevras
il	recevra
nous	recevrons
vous	recevrez
ils	recevront

IMPERATIVE		*CONDITIONAL*	
reçois		je	recevrais
recevons		tu	recevrais
recevez		il	recevrait
		nous	recevrions
		vous	recevriez
		ils	recevraient

to receive

PAST HISTORIC		PRESENT SUBJUNCTIVE	
je	reçus	je	reçoive
tu	reçus	tu	reçoives
il	reçut	il	reçoive
nous	reçûmes	nous	recevions
vous	reçûtes	vous	receviez
ils	reçurent	ils	reçoivent

PERFECT		PAST SUBJUNCTIVE	
j'	ai reçu	je	reçusse
tu	as reçu	tu	reçusses
il	a reçu	il	reçût
nous	avons reçu	nous	reçussions
vous	avez reçu	vous	reçussiez
ils	ont reçu	ils	reçussent

CONSTRUCTIONS

recevoir un cadeau de qn to receive a present from sb
être reçu à un examen to pass an exam
être reçu à l'université to get a place at university
il a reçu un coup de pied he got kicked

82 rendre

to give back

PRESENT PARTICIPLE
rendant

PAST PARTICIPLE
rendu

PRESENT		*IMPERFECT*	
je	**rends**	je	**rendais**
tu	**rends**	tu	**rendais**
il	**rend**	il	**rendait**
nous	**rendons**	nous	**rendions**
vous	**rendez**	vous	**rendiez**
ils	**rendent**	ils	**rendaient**

		FUTURE	
		je	**rendrai**
		tu	**rendras**
		il	**rendra**
		nous	**rendrons**
		vous	**rendrez**
		ils	**rendront**

IMPERATIVE	*CONDITIONAL*	
rends	je	**rendrais**
rendons	tu	**rendrais**
rendez	il	**rendrait**
	nous	**rendrions**
	vous	**rendriez**
	ils	**rendraient**

PAST HISTORIC		PRESENT SUBJUNCTIVE	
je	rendis	je	rende
tu	rendis	tu	rendes
il	rendit	il	rende
nous	rendîmes	nous	rendions
vous	rendîtes	vous	rendiez
ils	rendirent	ils	rendent
PERFECT		**PAST SUBJUNCTIVE**	
j'	ai rendu	je	rendisse
tu	as rendu	tu	rendisses
il	a rendu	il	rendît
nous	avons rendu	nous	rendissions
vous	avez rendu	vous	rendissiez
ils	ont rendu	ils	rendissent

CONSTRUCTIONS

rendre qch à qn to give sth back to sb
rendre qn heureux to make sb happy
rendre visite à qn to pay sb a visit
se rendre to surrender
se rendre compte de qch to realize sth

83 rentrer
to go back; to go in

PRESENT PARTICIPLE
rentrant

PAST PARTICIPLE
rentré

PRESENT		*IMPERFECT*	
je	**rentre**	je	**rentrais**
tu	**rentres**	tu	**rentrais**
il	**rentre**	il	**rentrait**
nous	**rentrons**	nous	**rentrions**
vous	**rentrez**	vous	**rentriez**
ils	**rentrent**	ils	**rentraient**

		FUTURE	
		je	**rentrerai**
		tu	**rentreras**
		il	**rentrera**
		nous	**rentrerons**
		vous	**rentrerez**
		ils	**rentreront**

IMPERATIVE		*CONDITIONAL*	
	rentre	je	**rentrerais**
	rentrons	tu	**rentrerais**
	rentrez	il	**rentrerait**
		nous	**rentrerions**
		vous	**rentreriez**
		ils	**rentreraient**

to go back; to go in

PAST HISTORIC		PRESENT SUBJUNCTIVE	
je	rentrai	je	rentre
tu	rentras	tu	rentres
il	rentra	il	rentre
nous	rentrâmes	nous	rentrions
vous	rentrâtes	vous	rentriez
ils	rentrèrent	ils	rentrent

PERFECT		PAST SUBJUNCTIVE	
je	suis rentré	je	rentrasse
tu	es rentré	tu	rentrasses
il	est rentré	il	rentrât
nous	sommes rentrés	nous	rentrassions
vous	êtes rentré(s)	vous	rentrassiez
ils	sont rentrés	ils	rentrassent

CONSTRUCTIONS
rentrer à la maison   to go back home
rentrer dans une firme   to join a firm
rentrer dans un arbre   to crash into a tree
il a rentré la voiture   he put the car away
rentrer ses griffes   to draw in one's claws

84 répondre
to answer

also **confondre**
to confuse

PRESENT PARTICIPLE
répondant

correspondre
to correspond

PAST PARTICIPLE
répondu

tondre
to shear

PRESENT		*IMPERFECT*	
je	réponds	je	répondais
tu	réponds	tu	répondais
il	répond	il	répondait
nous	répondons	nous	répondions
vous	répondez	vous	répondiez
ils	répondent	ils	répondaient

		FUTURE	
		je	répondrai
		tu	répondras
		il	répondra
		nous	répondrons
		vous	répondrez
		ils	répondront

IMPERATIVE		*CONDITIONAL*	
	réponds	je	répondrais
	répondons	tu	répondrais
	répondez	il	répondrait
		nous	répondrions
		vous	répondriez
		ils	répondraient

PAST HISTORIC		PRESENT SUBJUNCTIVE	
je	répondis	je	réponde
tu	répondis	tu	répondes
il	répondit	il	réponde
nous	répondîmes	nous	répondions
vous	répondîtes	vous	répondiez
ils	répondirent	ils	répondent

PERFECT		PAST SUBJUNCTIVE	
j'	ai répondu	je	répondisse
tu	as répondu	tu	répondisses
il	a répondu	il	répondît
nous	avons répondu	nous	répondissions
vous	avez répondu	vous	répondissiez
ils	ont répondu	ils	répondissent

CONSTRUCTIONS

répondre à qn/à une question   to answer sb/a question
on a sonné – va répondre   that's the bell – go and answer the door
ça ne répond pas   there's no reply
répondre de qn   to answer for sb

85 résoudre

to solve

PRESENT PARTICIPLE
résolvant

PAST PARTICIPLE
résolu

PRESENT		*IMPERFECT*	
je	**résous**	je	**résolvais**
tu	**résous**	tu	**résolvais**
il	**résout**	il	**résolvait**
nous	**résolvons**	nous	**résolvions**
vous	**résolvez**	vous	**résolviez**
ils	**résolvent**	ils	**résolvaient**

		FUTURE	
		je	**résoudrai**
		tu	**résoudras**
		il	**résoudra**
		nous	**résoudrons**
		vous	**résoudrez**
		ils	**résoudront**

IMPERATIVE	*CONDITIONAL*	
résous	je	**résoudrais**
résolvons	tu	**résoudrais**
résolvez	il	**résoudrait**
	nous	**résoudrions**
	vous	**résoudriez**
	ils	**résoudraient**

PAST HISTORIC		PRESENT SUBJUNCTIVE	
je	résolus	je	résolve
tu	résolus	tu	résolves
il	résolut	il	résolve
nous	résolûmes	nous	résolvions
vous	résolûtes	vous	résolviez
ils	résolurent	ils	résolvent

PERFECT		PAST SUBJUNCTIVE	
j'	ai résolu	je	résolusse
tu	as résolu	tu	résolusses
il	a résolu	il	résolût
nous	avons résolu	nous	résolussions
vous	avez résolu	vous	résolussiez
ils	ont résolu	ils	résolussent

CONSTRUCTIONS
se résoudre à faire qch to resolve to do sth
être résolu à faire to be set on doing

86 rester
to remain

PRESENT PARTICIPLE
restant

PAST PARTICIPLE
resté

PRESENT
je	reste
tu	restes
il	reste
nous	restons
vous	restez
ils	restent

IMPERFECT
je	restais
tu	restais
il	restait
nous	restions
vous	restiez
ils	restaient

FUTURE
je	resterai
tu	resteras
il	restera
nous	resterons
vous	resterez
ils	resteront

IMPERATIVE
reste
restons
restez

CONDITIONAL
je	resterais
tu	resterais
il	resterait
nous	resterions
vous	resteriez
ils	resteraient

PAST HISTORIC		PRESENT SUBJUNCTIVE	
je	restai	je	reste
tu	restas	tu	restes
il	resta	il	reste
nous	restâmes	nous	restions
vous	restâtes	vous	restiez
ils	restèrent	ils	restent

PERFECT		PAST SUBJUNCTIVE	
je	suis resté	je	restasse
tu	es resté	tu	restasses
il	est resté	il	restât
nous	sommes restés	nous	restassions
vous	êtes resté(s)	vous	restassiez
ils	sont restés	ils	restassent

CONSTRUCTIONS
il est resté à regarder la télévision   he stayed watching
television
c'est tout l'argent qui leur reste   that's all the money they
have left
il reste encore un peu de pain   there's still a little bread
left

87 retourner
to return

PRESENT PARTICIPLE
retournant

PAST PARTICIPLE
retourné

PRESENT		IMPERFECT	
je	**retourne**	je	**retournais**
tu	**retournes**	tu	**retournais**
il	**retourne**	il	**retournait**
nous	**retournons**	nous	**retournions**
vous	**retournez**	vous	**retourniez**
ils	**retournent**	ils	**retournaient**

		FUTURE	
		je	**retournerai**
		tu	**retourneras**
		il	**retournera**
		nous	**retournerons**
		vous	**retournerez**
		ils	**retourneront**

IMPERATIVE		CONDITIONAL	
	retourne	je	**retournerais**
	retournons	tu	**retournerais**
	retournez	il	**retournerait**
		nous	**retournerions**
		vous	**retourneriez**
		ils	**retourneraient**

retourner 87

to return

PAST HISTORIC		PRESENT SUBJUNCTIVE	
je	retournai	je	retourne
tu	retournas	tu	retournes
il	retourna	il	retourne
nous	retournâmes	nous	retournions
vous	retournâtes	vous	retourniez
ils	retournèrent	ils	retournent

PERFECT		PAST SUBJUNCTIVE	
je	suis retourné	je	retournasse
tu	es retourné	tu	retournasses
il	est retourné	il	retournât
nous	sommes retournés	nous	retournassions
vous	êtes retourné(s)	vous	retournassiez
ils	sont retournés	ils	retournassent

CONSTRUCTIONS

il a retourné le seau/sac he turned the bucket upside down/the bag inside out

il a retourné les marchandises he sent the goods back

retourner en Italie to go back to Italy

se retourner to turn over; to turn round

88 revenir

to come back

PRESENT PARTICIPLE
revenant

PAST PARTICIPLE
revenu

PRESENT		IMPERFECT	
je	**reviens**	je	**revenais**
tu	**reviens**	tu	**revenais**
il	**revient**	il	**revenait**
nous	**revenons**	nous	**revenions**
vous	**revenez**	vous	**reveniez**
ils	**reviennent**	ils	**revenaient**

		FUTURE	
		je	**reviendrai**
		tu	**reviendras**
		il	**reviendra**
		nous	**reviendrons**
		vous	**reviendrez**
		ils	**reviendront**

IMPERATIVE	CONDITIONAL	
reviens	je	**reviendrais**
revenons	tu	**reviendrais**
revenez	il	**reviendrait**
	nous	**reviendrions**
	vous	**reviendriez**
	ils	**reviendraient**

revenir 88
to come back

PAST HISTORIC		PRESENT SUBJUNCTIVE	
je	revins	je	revienne
tu	revins	tu	reviennes
il	revint	il	revienne
nous	revînmes	nous	revenions
vous	revîntes	vous	reveniez
ils	revinrent	ils	reviennent

PERFECT		PAST SUBJUNCTIVE	
je	suis revenu	je	revinsse
tu	es revenu	tu	revinsses
il	est revenu	il	revînt
nous	sommes revenus	nous	revinssions
vous	êtes revenu(s)	vous	revinssiez
ils	sont revenus	ils	revinssent

CONSTRUCTIONS
le repas revient à 70 F   the meal comes to 70 F
il est revenu à Paris   he came back to Paris
il est revenu de Paris   he's back from Paris
revenir sur une promesse   to go back on a promise
revenir sur ses pas   to retrace one's steps

89 rire

to laugh   *also* **sourire**
                            to smile

PRESENT PARTICIPLE
riant

PAST PARTICIPLE
ri

PRESENT		IMPERFECT	
je	ris	je	riais
tu	ris	tu	riais
il	rit	il	riait
nous	rions	nous	riions
vous	riez	vous	riiez
ils	rient	ils	riaient

FUTURE

je	rirai
tu	riras
il	rira
nous	rirons
vous	rirez
ils	riront

IMPERATIVE	CONDITIONAL	
ris	je	rirais
rions	tu	rirais
riez	il	rirait
	nous	ririons
	vous	ririez
	ils	riraient

PAST HISTORIC	PRESENT SUBJUNCTIVE
je ris	je rie
tu ris	tu ries
il rit	il rie
nous rîmes	nous riions
vous rîtes	vous riiez
ils rirent	ils rient

PERFECT	PAST SUBJUNCTIVE
j' ai ri	je risse
tu as ri	tu risses
il a ri	il rît
nous avons ri	nous rissions
vous avez ri	vous rissiez
ils ont ri	ils rissent

CONSTRUCTIONS
rire de qn/qch to laugh at sb/sth
il a fait cela pour rire he did it for a joke
rire aux éclats to roar with laughter

90 rompre
to break

also **corrompre**
to corrupt

PRESENT PARTICIPLE
rompant

interrompre
to interrupt

PAST PARTICIPLE
rompu

PRESENT		IMPERFECT	
je	romps	je	rompais
tu	romps	tu	rompais
il	rompt	il	rompait
nous	rompons	nous	rompions
vous	rompez	vous	rompiez
ils	rompent	ils	rompaient

FUTURE	
je	romprai
tu	rompras
il	rompra
nous	romprons
vous	romprez
ils	rompront

IMPERATIVE	CONDITIONAL	
romps	je	romprais
rompons	tu	romprais
rompez	il	romprait
	nous	romprions
	vous	rompriez
	ils	rompraient

PAST HISTORIC		PRESENT SUBJUNCTIVE	
je	rompis	je	rompe
tu	rompis	tu	rompes
il	rompit	il	rompe
nous	rompîmes	nous	rompions
vous	rompîtes	vous	rompiez
ils	rompirent	ils	rompent

PERFECT		PAST SUBJUNCTIVE	
j'	ai rompu	je	rompisse
tu	as rompu	tu	rompisses
il	a rompu	il	rompît
nous	avons rompu	nous	rompissions
vous	avez rompu	vous	rompissiez
ils	ont rompu	ils	rompissent

CONSTRUCTIONS
ils ont rompu (leurs fiançailles)   they've broken off their engagement
rompre les rangs to fall out
se rompre to break; to burst
être rompu (de fatigue)   to be exhausted

91 savoir
to know

PRESENT PARTICIPLE
sachant

PAST PARTICIPLE
su

PRESENT		IMPERFECT	
je	**sais**	je	**savais**
tu	**sais**	tu	**savais**
il	**sait**	il	**savait**
nous	**savons**	nous	**savions**
vous	**savez**	vous	**saviez**
ils	**savent**	ils	**savaient**

		FUTURE	
		je	**saurai**
		tu	**sauras**
		il	**saura**
		nous	**saurons**
		vous	**saurez**
		ils	**sauront**

IMPERATIVE	CONDITIONAL	
sache	je	**saurais**
sachons	tu	**saurais**
sachez	il	**saurait**
	nous	**saurions**
	vous	**sauriez**
	ils	**sauraient**

PAST HISTORIC		PRESENT SUBJUNCTIVE	
je	sus	je	sache
tu	sus	tu	saches
il	sut	il	sache
nous	sûmes	nous	sachions
vous	sûtes	vous	sachiez
ils	surent	ils	sachent
PERFECT		**PAST SUBJUNCTIVE**	
j'	ai su	je	susse
tu	as su	tu	susses
il	a su	il	sût
nous	avons su	nous	sussions
vous	avez su	vous	sussiez
ils	ont su	ils	sussent

CONSTRUCTIONS

savoir faire to know how to do; to be able to do
je ne sais pas quoi faire I don't know what to do
je vous ferai savoir I'll let you know
à savoir that is, namely
on ne sait jamais you never can tell

92 sentir

to smell; to feel   *also* **consentir**
                          to agree

PRESENT PARTICIPLE
sentant   **démentir**
                          to deny

PAST PARTICIPLE
senti   **mentir**
                          to lie

PRESENT		*IMPERFECT*	
je	sens	je	sentais
tu	sens	tu	sentais
il	sent	il	sentait
nous	sentons	nous	sentions
vous	sentez	vous	sentiez
ils	sentent	ils	sentaient

		FUTURE	
		je	sentirai
		tu	sentiras
		il	sentira
		nous	sentirons
		vous	sentirez
		ils	sentiront

IMPERATIVE		*CONDITIONAL*	
	sens	je	sentirais
	sentons	tu	sentirais
	sentez	il	sentirait
		nous	sentirions
		vous	sentiriez
		ils	sentiraient

to smell; to feel

ressentir
to feel

PAST HISTORIC		PRESENT SUBJUNCTIVE	
je	sentis	je	sente
tu	sentis	tu	sentes
il	sentit	il	sente
nous	sentîmes	nous	sentions
vous	sentîtes	vous	sentiez
ils	sentirent	ils	sentent

PERFECT		PAST SUBJUNCTIVE	
j'	ai senti	je	sentisse
tu	as senti	tu	sentisses
il	a senti	il	sentît
nous	avons senti	nous	sentissions
vous	avez senti	vous	sentissiez
ils	ont senti	ils	sentissent

CONSTRUCTIONS
sentir bon/mauvais to smell good *or* nice/bad
j'ai senti s'arrêter la voiture I felt the car stopping
se sentir mal/mieux to feel ill/better

93 servir

to serve

PRESENT PARTICIPLE
servant

PAST PARTICIPLE
servi

PRESENT		*IMPERFECT*	
je	**sers**	je	**servais**
tu	**sers**	tu	**servais**
il	**sert**	il	**servait**
nous	**servons**	nous	**servions**
vous	**servez**	vous	**serviez**
ils	**servent**	ils	**servaient**

		FUTURE	
		je	**servirai**
		tu	**serviras**
		il	**servira**
		nous	**servirons**
		vous	**servirez**
		ils	**serviront**

IMPERATIVE		*CONDITIONAL*	
	sers	je	**servirais**
	servons	tu	**servirais**
	servez	il	**servirait**
		nous	**servirions**
		vous	**serviriez**
		ils	**serviraient**

PAST HISTORIC		PRESENT SUBJUNCTIVE	
je	servis	je	serve
tu	servis	tu	serves
il	servit	il	serve
nous	servîmes	nous	servions
vous	servîtes	vous	serviez
ils	servirent	ils	servent

PERFECT		PAST SUBJUNCTIVE	
j'	ai servi	je	servisse
tu	as servi	tu	servisses
il	a servi	il	servît
nous	avons servi	nous	servissions
vous	avez servi	vous	servissiez
ils	ont servi	ils	servissent

CONSTRUCTIONS

servir un plat à qn   to serve sb with a dish
servir à qn/à qch   to be useful to sb/for sth
servir à faire   to be used for doing
à quoi sert de pleurer?   what's the use of crying?
servir de   to act as; to serve as
se servir d'un plat   to help oneself to a dish

94 songer
to think

PRESENT PARTICIPLE
songeant

PAST PARTICIPLE
songé

also **plonger**
to dive

prolonger
to prolong

rallonger
to lengthen

PRESENT		IMPERFECT	
je	songe	je	songeais
tu	songes	tu	songeais
il	songe	il	songeait
nous	songeons	nous	songions
vous	songez	vous	songiez
ils	songent	ils	songeaient

FUTURE
je	songerai
tu	songeras
il	songera
nous	songerons
vous	songerez
ils	songeront

IMPERATIVE
songe
songeons
songez

CONDITIONAL
je	songerais
tu	songerais
il	songerait
nous	songerions
vous	songeriez
ils	songeraient

ronger
to gnaw

PAST HISTORIC		PRESENT SUBJUNCTIVE	
je	songeai	je	songe
tu	songeas	tu	songes
il	songea	il	songe
nous	songeâmes	nous	songions
vous	songeâtes	vous	songiez
ils	songèrent	ils	songent

PERFECT		PAST SUBJUNCTIVE	
j'	ai songé	je	songeasse
tu	as songé	tu	songeasses
il	a songé	il	songeât
nous	avons songé	nous	songeassions
vous	avez songé	vous	songeassiez
ils	ont songé	ils	songeassent

CONSTRUCTIONS
songer à qch to think sth over; to think of sth
songer à faire qch to contemplate doing sth

95 sortir

to go out

also **ressortir**
to stand out

PRESENT PARTICIPLE
sortant

PAST PARTICIPLE
sorti

PRESENT	
je	**sors**
tu	**sors**
il	**sort**
nous	**sortons**
vous	**sortez**
ils	**sortent**

IMPERFECT	
je	**sortais**
tu	**sortais**
il	**sortait**
nous	**sortions**
vous	**sortiez**
ils	**sortaient**

FUTURE	
je	**sortirai**
tu	**sortiras**
il	**sortira**
nous	**sortirons**
vous	**sortirez**
ils	**sortiront**

IMPERATIVE	
	sors
	sortons
	sortez

CONDITIONAL	
je	**sortirais**
tu	**sortirais**
il	**sortirait**
nous	**sortirions**
vous	**sortiriez**
ils	**sortiraient**

PAST HISTORIC		PRESENT SUBJUNCTIVE	
je	sortis	je	sorte
tu	sortis	tu	sortes
il	sortit	il	sorte
nous	sortîmes	nous	sortions
vous	sortîtes	vous	sortiez
ils	sortirent	ils	sortent

PERFECT		PAST SUBJUNCTIVE	
je	suis sorti	je	sortisse
tu	es sorti	tu	sortisses
il	est sorti	il	sortît
nous	sommes sortis	nous	sortissions
vous	êtes sorti(s)	vous	sortissiez
ils	sont sortis	ils	sortissent

CONSTRUCTIONS

sortir d'une pièce/d'un pays to go (*or* come) out of a
room/leave a country
il a sorti la voiture du garage he got the car out of the
garage
sortir le chien to take the dog out

96 se souvenir
to remember

PRESENT PARTICIPLE
se souvenant

PAST PARTICIPLE
souvenu

PRESENT		*IMPERFECT*	
je	me souviens	je	me souvenais
tu	te souviens	tu	te souvenais
il	se souvient	il	se souvenait
nous	nous souvenons	nous	nous souvenions
vous	vous souvenez	vous	vous souveniez
ils	se souviennent	ils	se souvenaient

FUTURE	
je	me souviendrai
tu	te souviendras
il	se souviendra
nous	nous souviendrons
vous	vous souviendrez
ils	se souviendront

IMPERATIVE	*CONDITIONAL*	
souviens-toi	je	me souviendrais
souvenons-nous	tu	te souviendrais
souvenez-vous	il	se souviendrait
	nous	nous souviendrions
	vous	vous souviendriez
	ils	se souviendraient

PAST HISTORIC		PRESENT SUBJUNCTIVE	
je	me souvins	je	me souvienne
tu	te souvins	tu	te souviennes
il	se souvint	il	se souvienne
nous	nous souvînmes	nous	nous souvenions
vous	vous souvîntes	vous	vous souveniez
ils	se souvinrent	ils	se souviennent

PERFECT		PAST SUBJUNCTIVE	
je	me suis souvenu	je	me souvinsse
tu	t'es souvenu	tu	te souvinsses
il	s'est souvenu	il	se souvînt
nous	nous sommes souvenus	nous	nous souvinssions
vous	vous êtes souvenu(s)	vous	vous souvinssiez
ils	se sont souvenus	ils	se souvinssent

CONSTRUCTIONS

se souvenir de qn/qch to remember sb/sth
se souvenir d'avoir fait qch to remember doing sth

97 suffire
to be enough

PRESENT PARTICIPLE
suffisant

PAST PARTICIPLE
suffi

PRESENT		*IMPERFECT*	
je	**suffis**	je	**suffisais**
tu	**suffis**	tu	**suffisais**
il	**suffit**	il	**suffisait**
nous	**suffisons**	nous	**suffisions**
vous	**suffisez**	vous	**suffisiez**
ils	**suffisent**	ils	**suffisaient**

		FUTURE	
		je	**suffirai**
		tu	**suffiras**
		il	**suffira**
		nous	**suffirons**
		vous	**suffirez**
		ils	**suffiront**

IMPERATIVE		*CONDITIONAL*	
	suffis	je	**suffirais**
	suffisons	tu	**suffirais**
	suffisez	il	**suffirait**
		nous	**suffirions**
		vous	**suffiriez**
		ils	**suffiraient**

PAST HISTORIC		PRESENT SUBJUNCTIVE	
je	suffis	je	suffise
tu	suffis	tu	suffises
il	suffit	il	suffise
nous	suffîmes	nous	suffisions
vous	suffîtes	vous	suffisiez
ils	suffirent	ils	suffisent

PERFECT		PAST SUBJUNCTIVE	
j'	ai suffi	je	suffisse
tu	as suffi	tu	suffisses
il	a suffi	il	suffît
nous	avons suffi	nous	suffissions
vous	avez suffi	vous	suffissiez
ils	ont suffi	ils	suffissent

CONSTRUCTIONS

suffire à or **pour faire**   to be sufficient or enough to do
suffire à qn   to be enough for sb
(ça) suffit!   that's enough!, that will do!
il suffit de 2 heures pour y aller   2 hours is enough to get there

98 suivre

to follow

also **poursuivre**
to pursue

PRESENT PARTICIPLE
suivant

PAST PARTICIPLE
suivi

PRESENT		IMPERFECT	
je	suis	je	suivais
tu	suis	tu	suivais
il	suit	il	suivait
nous	suivons	nous	suivions
vous	suivez	vous	suiviez
ils	suivent	ils	suivaient

		FUTURE	
		je	suivrai
		tu	suivras
		il	suivra
		nous	suivrons
		vous	suivrez
		ils	suivront

IMPERATIVE	CONDITIONAL	
suis	je	suivrais
suivons	tu	suivrais
suivez	il	suivrait
	nous	suivrions
	vous	suivriez
	ils	suivraient

PAST HISTORIC		PRESENT SUBJUNCTIVE	
je	suivis	je	suive
tu	suivis	tu	suives
il	suivit	il	suive
nous	suivîmes	nous	suivions
vous	suivîtes	vous	suiviez
ils	suivirent	ils	suivent

PERFECT		PAST SUBJUNCTIVE	
j'	ai suivi	je	suivisse
tu	as suivi	tu	suivisses
il	a suivi	il	suivît
nous	avons suivi	nous	suivissions
vous	avez suivi	vous	suivissiez
ils	ont suivi	ils	suivissent

CONSTRUCTIONS

suivre un régime   to be on a diet
suivre une classe   to attend a class
faire suivre son courrier   to have one's mail forwarded

99 surseoir
to defer

PRESENT PARTICIPLE
sursoyant

PAST PARTICIPLE
sursis

PRESENT		*IMPERFECT*	
je	**sursois**	je	**sursoyais**
tu	**sursois**	tu	**sursoyais**
il	**sursoit**	il	**sursoyait**
nous	**sursoyons**	nous	**sursoyions**
vous	**sursoyez**	vous	**sursoyiez**
ils	**sursoient**	ils	**sursoyaient**

		FUTURE	
		je	**surseoirai**
		tu	**surseoiras**
		il	**surseoira**
		nous	**surseoirons**
		vous	**surseoirez**
		ils	**surseoiront**

IMPERATIVE		*CONDITIONAL*	
	sursois	je	**surseoirais**
	sursoyons	tu	**surseoirais**
	sursoyez	il	**surseoirait**
		nous	**surseoirions**
		vous	**surseoiriez**
		ils	**surseoiraient**

surseoir 99
to defer

PAST HISTORIC		PRESENT SUBJUNCTIVE	
je	sursis	je	sursoie
tu	sursis	tu	sursoies
il	sursit	il	sursoie
nous	sursîmes	nous	sursoyions
vous	sursîtes	vous	sursoyiez
ils	sursirent	ils	sursoient

PERFECT		PAST SUBJUNCTIVE	
j'	ai sursis	je	sursisse
tu	as sursis	tu	sursisses
il	a sursis	il	sursît
nous	avons sursis	nous	sursissions
vous	avez sursis	vous	sursissiez
ils	ont sursis	ils	sursissent

CONSTRUCTIONS
surseoir à qch   to defer *or* postpone sth

100 se taire
to stop talking

PRESENT PARTICIPLE
se taisant

PAST PARTICIPLE
tu

PRESENT		IMPERFECT	
je	me tais	je	me taisais
tu	te tais	tu	te taisais
il	se tait	il	se taisait
nous	nous taisons	nous	nous taisions
vous	vous taisez	vous	vous taisiez
ils	se taisent	ils	se taisaient

		FUTURE	
		je	me tairai
		tu	te tairas
		il	se taira
		nous	nous tairons
		vous	vous tairez
		ils	se tairont

IMPERATIVE		CONDITIONAL	
	tais-toi	je	me tairais
	taisons-nous	tu	te tairais
	taisez-vous	il	se tairait
		nous	nous tairions
		vous	vous tairiez
		ils	se tairaient

PAST HISTORIC		PRESENT SUBJUNCTIVE	
je	me tus	je	me taise
tu	te tus	tu	te taises
il	se tut	il	se taise
nous	nous tûmes	nous	nous taisions
vous	vous tûtes	vous	vous taisiez
ils	se turent	ils	se taisent

PERFECT		PAST SUBJUNCTIVE	
je	me suis tu	je	me tusse
tu	t'es tu	tu	te tusses
il	s'est tu	il	se tût
nous	nous sommes tus	nous	nous tussions
vous	vous êtes tu(s)	vous	vous tussiez
ils	se sont tus	ils	se tussent

CONSTRUCTIONS
ils se sont tus they stopped talking
taisez-vous! be quiet!
se taire sur qch to keep quiet about sth

101 tenir

to hold

also **appartenir**
to belong

PRESENT PARTICIPLE
tenant

contenir
to contain

PAST PARTICIPLE
tenu

entretenir
to maintain

PRESENT		*IMPERFECT*	
je	tiens	je	tenais
tu	tiens	tu	tenais
il	tient	il	tenait
nous	tenons	nous	tenions
vous	tenez	vous	teniez
ils	tiennent	ils	tenaient

FUTURE	
je	tiendrai
tu	tiendras
il	tiendra
nous	tiendrons
vous	tiendrez
ils	tiendront

IMPERATIVE		*CONDITIONAL*	
	tiens	je	tiendrais
	tenons	tu	tiendrais
	tenez	il	tiendrait
		nous	tiendrions
		vous	tiendriez
		ils	tiendraient

to hold

soutenir
to support

PAST HISTORIC		PRESENT SUBJUNCTIVE	
je	tins	je	tienne
tu	tins	tu	tiennes
il	tint	il	tienne
nous	tînmes	nous	tenions
vous	tîntes	vous	teniez
ils	tinrent	ils	tiennent

PERFECT		PAST SUBJUNCTIVE	
j'	ai tenu	je	tinsse
tu	as tenu	tu	tinsses
il	a tenu	il	tînt
nous	avons tenu	nous	tinssions
vous	avez tenu	vous	tinssiez
ils	ont tenu	ils	tinssent

CONSTRUCTIONS

tenir à   to be attached to; to care about
tenir à faire   to be keen to do
il ne tient qu'à vous de décider   it's up to you to decide
se tenir   to stand; to take place
être tenu de faire   to be obliged to do

102 tomber

to fall

also **retomber**

to fall back

PRESENT PARTICIPLE
tombant

PAST PARTICIPLE
tombé

PRESENT

je	tombe
tu	tombes
il	tombe
nous	tombons
vous	tombez
ils	tombent

IMPERATIVE

tombe
tombons
tombez

IMPERFECT

je	tombais
tu	tombais
il	tombait
nous	tombions
vous	tombiez
ils	tombaient

FUTURE

je	tomberai
tu	tomberas
il	tombera
nous	tomberons
vous	tomberez
ils	tomberont

CONDITIONAL

je	tomberais
tu	tomberais
il	tomberait
nous	tomberions
vous	tomberiez
ils	tomberaient

to fall

PAST HISTORIC		PRESENT SUBJUNCTIVE	
je	tombai	je	tombe
tu	tombas	tu	tombes
il	tomba	il	tombe
nous	tombâmes	nous	tombions
vous	tombâtes	vous	tombiez
ils	tombèrent	ils	tombent

PERFECT		PAST SUBJUNCTIVE	
je	suis tombé	je	tombasse
tu	es tombé	tu	tombasses
il	est tombé	il	tombât
nous	sommes tombés	nous	tombassions
vous	êtes tombé(s)	vous	tombassiez
ils	sont tombés	ils	tombassent

CONSTRUCTIONS

tomber de bicyclette / cheval to fall off one's bicycle / horse
laisser tomber qch to drop sth
faire tomber to knock over; to knock down
tomber malade / amoureux to fall ill / in love
tomber sur to come across

103 traduire
to translate

PRESENT PARTICIPLE
traduisant

PAST PARTICIPLE
traduit

PRESENT		IMPERFECT	
je	**traduis**	je	**traduisais**
tu	**traduis**	tu	**traduisais**
il	**traduit**	il	**traduisait**
nous	**traduisons**	nous	**traduisions**
vous	**traduisez**	vous	**traduisiez**
ils	**traduisent**	ils	**traduisaient**

		FUTURE	
		je	**traduirai**
		tu	**traduiras**
		il	**traduira**
		nous	**traduirons**
		vous	**traduirez**
		ils	**traduiront**

IMPERATIVE		CONDITIONAL	
	traduis	je	**traduirais**
	traduisons	tu	**traduirais**
	traduisez	il	**traduirait**
		nous	**traduirions**
		vous	**traduiriez**
		ils	**traduiraient**

PAST HISTORIC		PRESENT SUBJUNCTIVE	
je	traduisis	je	traduise
tu	traduisis	tu	traduises
il	traduisit	il	traduise
nous	traduisîmes	nous	traduisions
vous	traduisîtes	vous	traduisiez
ils	traduisirent	ils	traduisent

PERFECT		PAST SUBJUNCTIVE	
j'	ai traduit	je	traduisisse
tu	as traduit	tu	traduisisses
il	a traduit	il	traduisît
nous	avons traduit	nous	traduisissions
vous	avez traduit	vous	traduisissiez
ils	ont traduit	ils	traduisissent

CONSTRUCTIONS
traduit en/du français translated into/from French

104 traire

to milk

PRESENT PARTICIPLE
trayant

PAST PARTICIPLE
trait

also **distraire**
to distract

extraire
to extract

soustraire
to subtract

PRESENT		IMPERFECT	
je	trais	je	trayais
tu	trais	tu	trayais
il	trait	il	trayait
nous	trayons	nous	trayions
vous	trayez	vous	trayiez
ils	traient	ils	trayaient

		FUTURE	
		je	trairai
		tu	trairas
		il	traira
		nous	trairons
		vous	trairez
		ils	trairont

IMPERATIVE	CONDITIONAL	
trais	je	trairais
trayons	tu	trairais
trayez	il	trairait
	nous	trairions
	vous	trairiez
	ils	trairaient

PAST HISTORIC not used	*PRESENT SUBJUNCTIVE* je traie tu traies il traie nous trayions vous trayiez ils traient
PERFECT j' ai trait tu as trait il a trait nous avons trait vous avez trait ils ont trait	*PAST SUBJUNCTIVE* not used

105 vaincre
to defeat

also **convaincre**
to convince

PRESENT PARTICIPLE
vainquant

PAST PARTICIPLE
vaincu

PRESENT

je	**vaincs**
tu	**vaincs**
il	**vainc**
nous	**vainquons**
vous	**vainquez**
ils	**vainquent**

IMPERFECT

je	**vainquais**
tu	**vainquais**
il	**vainquait**
nous	**vainquions**
vous	**vainquiez**
ils	**vainquaient**

FUTURE

je	**vaincrai**
tu	**vaincras**
il	**vaincra**
nous	**vaincrons**
vous	**vaincrez**
ils	**vaincront**

IMPERATIVE

vaincs
vainquons
vainquez

CONDITIONAL

je	**vaincrais**
tu	**vaincrais**
il	**vaincrait**
nous	**vaincrions**
vous	**vaincriez**
ils	**vaincraient**

PAST HISTORIC		PRESENT SUBJUNCTIVE	
je	vainquis	je	vainque
tu	vainquis	tu	vainques
il	vainquit	il	vainque
nous	vainquîmes	nous	vainquions
vous	vainquîtes	vous	vainquiez
ils	vainquirent	ils	vainquent

PERFECT		PAST SUBJUNCTIVE	
j'	ai vaincu	je	vainquisse
tu	as vaincu	tu	vainquisses
il	a vaincu	il	vainquît
nous	avons vaincu	nous	vainquissions
vous	avez vaincu	vous	vainquissiez
ils	ont vaincu	ils	vainquissent

CONSTRUCTIONS
s'avouer vaincu to admit defeat

106 valoir

to be worth

PRESENT PARTICIPLE
valant

PAST PARTICIPLE
valu

PRESENT		*IMPERFECT*	
je	**vaux**	je	**valais**
tu	**vaux**	tu	**valais**
il	**vaut**	il	**valait**
nous	**valons**	nous	**valions**
vous	**valez**	vous	**valiez**
ils	**valent**	ils	**valaient**

		FUTURE	
		je	**vaudrai**
		tu	**vaudras**
		il	**vaudra**
		nous	**vaudrons**
		vous	**vaudrez**
		ils	**vaudront**

IMPERATIVE		*CONDITIONAL*	
	vaux	je	**vaudrais**
	valons	tu	**vaudrais**
	valez	il	**vaudrait**
		nous	**vaudrions**
		vous	**vaudriez**
		ils	**vaudraient**

PAST HISTORIC		PRESENT SUBJUNCTIVE	
je	valus	je	vaille
tu	valus	tu	vailles
il	valut	il	vaille
nous	valûmes	nous	valions
vous	valûtes	vous	valiez
ils	valurent	ils	vaillent

PERFECT		PAST SUBJUNCTIVE	
j'	ai valu	je	valusse
tu	as valu	tu	valusses
il	a valu	il	valût
nous	avons valu	nous	valussions
vous	avez valu	vous	valussiez
ils	ont valu	ils	valussent

CONSTRUCTIONS

valoir cher / 10 F to be worth a lot / 10 F
cet outil ne vaut rien this tool is useless
il vaut mieux se taire it's better to say nothing
ce film vaut la peine d'être vu this film is worth seeing

107 vendre
to sell

also **défendre**
to defend

PRESENT PARTICIPLE
vendant

dépendre
to depend

PAST PARTICIPLE
vendu

entendre
to hear

PRESENT		*IMPERFECT*	
je	vends	je	vendais
tu	vends	tu	vendais
il	vend	il	vendait
nous	vendons	nous	vendions
vous	vendez	vous	vendiez
ils	vendent	ils	vendaient

		FUTURE	
		je	vendrai
		tu	vendras
		il	vendra
		nous	vendrons
		vous	vendrez
		ils	vendront

IMPERATIVE		*CONDITIONAL*	
	vends	je	vendrais
	vendons	tu	vendrais
	vendez	il	vendrait
		nous	vendrions
		vous	vendriez
		ils	vendraient

to sell

pendre
   to hang

répandre
   to spread

tendre
   to stretch

PAST HISTORIC		PRESENT SUBJUNCTIVE	
je	vendis	je	vende
tu	vendis	tu	vendes
il	vendît	il	vende
nous	vendîmes	nous	vendions
vous	vendîtes	vous	vendiez
ils	vendirent	ils	vendent

PERFECT		PAST SUBJUNCTIVE	
j'	ai vendu	je	vendisse
tu	as vendu	tu	vendisses
il	a vendu	il	vendît
nous	avons vendu	nous	vendissions
vous	avez vendu	vous	vendissiez
ils	ont vendu	ils	vendissent

CONSTRUCTIONS
vendre qch à qn   to sell sb sth
il me l'a vendu 10 F   he sold it to me for 10 F
'à vendre'   'for sale'
ils se vendent à la pièce / douzaine   they are sold
singly / by the dozen

108 venir

to come

also **intervenir**
to intervene

PRESENT PARTICIPLE
venant

parvenir
to succeed

PAST PARTICIPLE
venu

survenir
to occur

PRESENT		*IMPERFECT*	
je	viens	je	venais
tu	viens	tu	venais
il	vient	il	venait
nous	venons	nous	venions
vous	venez	vous	veniez
ils	viennent	ils	venaient

		FUTURE	
		je	viendrai
		tu	viendras
		il	viendra
		nous	viendrons
		vous	viendrez
		ils	viendront

IMPERATIVE		*CONDITIONAL*	
	viens	je	viendrais
	venons	tu	viendrais
	venez	il	viendrait
		nous	viendrions
		vous	viendriez
		ils	viendraient

PAST HISTORIC		PRESENT SUBJUNCTIVE	
je	vins	je	vienne
tu	vins	tu	viennes
il	vint	il	vienne
nous	vînmes	nous	venions
vous	vîntes	vous	veniez
ils	vinrent	ils	viennent

PERFECT		PAST SUBJUNCTIVE	
je	suis venu	je	vinsse
tu	es venu	tu	vinsses
il	est venu	il	vînt
nous	sommes venus	nous	vinssions
vous	êtes venu(s)	vous	vinssiez
ils	sont venus	ils	vinssent

CONSTRUCTIONS

venir de Paris   to come from Paris
faire venir qn   to call *or* send for sb
venir de faire qch   to have just done sth
en venir à faire qch   to be reduced to doing sth

109 vêtir

to dress   *also* **revêtir**
to put on

PRESENT PARTICIPLE
vêtant

PAST PARTICIPLE
vêtu

PRESENT		IMPERFECT	
je	vêts	je	vêtais
tu	vêts	tu	vêtais
il	vêt	il	vêtait
nous	vêtons	nous	vêtions
vous	vêtez	vous	vêtiez
ils	vêtent	ils	vêtaient

		FUTURE	
		je	vêtirai
		tu	vêtiras
		il	vêtira
		nous	vêtirons
		vous	vêtirez
		ils	vêtiront

IMPERATIVE		CONDITIONAL	
	vêts	je	vêtirais
	vêtons	tu	vêtirais
	vêtez	il	vêtirait
		nous	vêtirions
		vous	vêtiriez
		ils	vêtiraient

PAST HISTORIC		PRESENT SUBJUNCTIVE	
je	vêtis	je	vête
tu	vêtis	tu	vêtes
il	vêtit	il	vête
nous	vêtîmes	nous	vêtions
vous	vêtîtes	vous	vêtiez
ils	vêtirent	ils	vêtent

PERFECT		PAST SUBJUNCTIVE	
j'	ai vêtu	je	vêtisse
tu	as vêtu	tu	vêtisses
il	a vêtu	il	vêtît
nous	avons vêtu	nous	vêtissions
vous	avez vêtu	vous	vêtissiez
ils	ont vêtu	ils	vêtissent

CONSTRUCTIONS
vêtu d'un pantalon et d'un chandail wearing trousers
and a sweater
se vêtir to dress

110 vivre

to live

also **survivre**
to survive

PRESENT PARTICIPLE
vivant

PAST PARTICIPLE
vécu

PRESENT		*IMPERFECT*	
je	vis	je	vivais
tu	vis	tu	vivais
il	vit	il	vivait
nous	vivons	nous	vivions
vous	vivez	vous	viviez
ils	vivent	ils	vivaient

		FUTURE	
		je	vivrai
		tu	vivras
		il	vivra
		nous	vivrons
		vous	vivrez
		ils	vivront

IMPERATIVE	*CONDITIONAL*	
vis	je	vivrais
vivons	tu	vivrais
vivez	il	vivrait
	nous	vivrions
	vous	vivriez
	ils	vivraient

PAST HISTORIC		PRESENT SUBJUNCTIVE	
je	vécus	je	vive
tu	vécus	tu	vives
il	vécut	il	vive
nous	vécûmes	nous	vivions
vous	vécûtes	vous	viviez
ils	vécurent	ils	vivent

PERFECT		PAST SUBJUNCTIVE	
j'	ai vécu	je	vécusse
tu	as vécu	tu	vécusses
il	a vécu	il	vécût
nous	avons vécu	nous	vécussions
vous	avez vécu	vous	vécussiez
ils	ont vécu	ils	vécussent

CONSTRUCTIONS

il vit à la campagne/en France he lives in the country/in France

vivre de rentes/légumes to live on a private income/on vegetables

il est facile/difficile à vivre he's easy/difficult to get on with

111 voir

to see

PRESENT PARTICIPLE
voyant

PAST PARTICIPLE
vu

also **entrevoir**
to catch a glimpse of

revoir
to revise

PRESENT
je	vois
tu	vois
il	voit
nous	voyons
vous	voyez
ils	voient

IMPERATIVE
vois
voyons
voyez

IMPERFECT
je	voyais
tu	voyais
il	voyait
nous	voyions
vous	voyiez
ils	voyaient

FUTURE
je	verrai
tu	verras
il	verra
nous	verrons
vous	verrez
ils	verront

CONDITIONAL
je	verrais
tu	verrais
il	verrait
nous	verrions
vous	verriez
ils	verraient

PAST HISTORIC		PRESENT SUBJUNCTIVE	
je	**vis**	je	**voie**
tu	**vis**	tu	**voies**
il	**vit**	il	**voie**
nous	**vîmes**	nous	**voyions**
vous	**vîtes**	vous	**voyiez**
ils	**virent**	ils	**voient**

PERFECT		PAST SUBJUNCTIVE	
j'	**ai vu**	je	**visse**
tu	**as vu**	tu	**visses**
il	**a vu**	il	**vît**
nous	**avons vu**	nous	**vissions**
vous	**avez vu**	vous	**vissiez**
ils	**ont vu**	ils	**vissent**

CONSTRUCTIONS

aller voir qn to go and see sb
faire voir qch to show sth
on verra bien we'll soon see
ça n'a rien à voir avec notre problème it's got nothing to do with our problem
voyons! come now!

112 vouloir
to want

PRESENT PARTICIPLE
voulant

PAST PARTICIPLE
voulu

PRESENT		*IMPERFECT*	
je	**veux**	je	**voulais**
tu	**veux**	tu	**voulais**
il	**veut**	il	**voulait**
nous	**voulons**	nous	**voulions**
vous	**voulez**	vous	**vouliez**
ils	**veulent**	ils	**voulaient**

		FUTURE	
		je	**voudrai**
		tu	**voudras**
		il	**voudra**
		nous	**voudrons**
		vous	**voudrez**
		ils	**voudront**

IMPERATIVE		*CONDITIONAL*	
	veuille	je	**voudrais**
	veuillons	tu	**voudrais**
	veuillez	il	**voudrait**
		nous	**voudrions**
		vous	**voudriez**
		ils	**voudraient**

PAST HISTORIC		PRESENT SUBJUNCTIVE	
je	voulus	je	veuille
tu	voulus	tu	veuilles
il	voulut	il	veuille
nous	voulûmes	nous	voulions
vous	voulûtes	vous	vouliez
ils	voulurent	ils	veuillent

PERFECT		PAST SUBJUNCTIVE	
j'	ai voulu	je	voulusse
tu	as voulu	tu	voulusses
il	a voulu	il	voulût
nous	avons voulu	nous	voulussions
vous	avez voulu	vous	voulussiez
ils	ont voulu	ils	voulussent

CONSTRUCTIONS

vouloir faire qch to want to do sth
je veux bien le faire I'm happy to do it; I don't mind doing it
en vouloir à qn to have something against sb
vouloir dire to mean

INDEX

(a) Each verb is numerically cross-referred to one of the 112 verb models shown in bold type. Defective verbs, however, are cross-referred to page 13.

(b) All entries are arranged in alphabetical order; for alphabetisation purposes, pronouns are not included: s'asseoir, se taire etc appear as asseoir (s'), taire (se) etc.

(c) With the exception of those verbs which are individually marked (see note (d)), and of Reflexive and Reciprocal verbs which are always conjugated with être, a verb's auxiliary is that of its verb model.

(d) Superior numbers refer you to notes on page 256, which outline how the verb deviates from its verb model.

(e) An asterisk (*) indicates that the verb is conjugated with être when intransitive and avoir when transitive.

abaisser	36	accuser	36	aider	36
abandonner	36	acharner (s')	36	aigrir	45
abattre	11	acheminer	36	aiguiser	36
abêtir	45	**acheter**	**1**	aimanter	36
abîmer	36	achever	52	aimer	36
abolir	45	**acquérir**	**2**	ajouter	36
abonder	36	actionner	36	ajuster	36
abonner	36	activer	36	alarmer	36
aborder	36	adapter	36	alerter	36
aboutir	45	additionner	36	alimenter	36
aboyer	63	adhérer	41	allécher	41
abréger	80	adjoindre	51	alléger	80
abreuver	36	admettre	56	alléguer	41
abriter	36	admirer	36	**aller**	**3**
abrutir	45	adopter	36	allier	25
absenter (s')	36	adorer	36	allumer	36
absorber	36	adosser	36	altérer	41
absoudre[4]	85	adoucir	45	alterner	36
abstenir (s')	101	adresser	36	alunir	45
abstraire	104	advenir[3]	108	amaigrir	45
abuser	36	aérer	41	ambitionner	36
accabler	36	affaiblir	45	améliorer	36
accaparer	36	affairer (s')	36	aménager	54
accéder	41	affaisser (s')	36	amener	52
accélérer	41	affamer	36	ameuter	36
accepter	36	affermir	45	amincir	45
accompagner	36	afficher	36	amoindrir	45
accomplir	45	affirmer	36	amollir	45
accorder	36	affliger	54	amonceler	4
accoter	36	affoler	36	amorcer	15
accoucher	36	affranchir	45	amorcer	15
accouder (s')	36	affréter	41	amplifier	25
accourir[5]	21	affronter	36	amputer	36
accoutumer	36	agacer	15	amuser	36
accrocher	36	agenouiller (s')	36	analyser	36
accroire	*page 13*	agir	45	anéantir	45
accroître[6]	27	agiter	36	angoisser	36
accroupir (s')	45	agrandir	45	animer	36
accueillir	28	agréer	24	annexer	36
accumuler	36	ahurir	45	annoncer	15
				annoter	36

annuler	36	assagir	45	avancer	15
anoblir	45	**assaillir**	7	avantager	54
anticiper	36	assainir	45	aventurer	36
apaiser	36	assassiner	36	avertir	45
apercevoir	81	assembler	36	aveugler	36
apitoyer	63	assener	52	avilir	45
aplatir	45	**asseoir (s')**	8	aviser	36
apparaître²	67	asservir	45	aviver	36
appareiller	36	assiéger	36	**avoir**	10
apparenter	36	assigner	36	avouer	36
apparier	36	assimiler	36	bâcler	36
apparoir	page 13	assister	36	bafouer	36
appartenir	101	associer	25	bagarrer (se)	36
appauvrir	45	assombrir	45	baigner	36
appeler	4	assommer	36	bâiller	36
applaudir	45	assortir	45	baiser	36
appliquer	36	assoupir	45	baisser	36
apporter	36	assouplir	45	balader (se)	36
apprécier	25	assourdir	45	balafrer	36
apprendre	5	assujettir	45	balancer	15
apprêter	36	assumer	36	balayer	70
apprivoiser	36	assurer	36	balbutier	25
approcher	36	astiquer	36	baliser	36
approfondir	45	astreindre	71	bannir	45
approprier	25	atermoyer	63	baptiser	36
approuver	36	attabler (s')	36	baratiner	36
appuyer	63	attacher	36	barbouiller	36
arc-bouter	36	attaquer	36	barioler	36
argenter	36	atteindre	71	barrer	36
arguer	36	atteler	4	barricader	36
armer	36	**attendre**	9	basculer	36
arpenter	36	attendrir	45	baser	36
arracher	36	atterrir	45	batailler	36
arranger	54	attirer	36	batifoler	36
arrêter	36	attraper	36	bâtir	45
arriver	6	attribuer	36	**battre**	11
arrondir	45	augmenter	36	bavarder	36
arroser	36	autoriser	36	baver	36
asphyxier	25	avachir (s')	45	bêcher	36
aspirer	36	avaler	36	becqueter	50

béer	*page 13*	bousiller	36	capturer	36
bégayer	70	boutonner	36	caractériser	36
bêler	36	braconner	36	caresser	36
bénéficier	25	brailler	36	caricaturer	36
bénir	45	braire[7]	104	caser	36
bercer	15	brancher	36	casser	36
berner	36	brandir	45	cataloguer	36
beugler	36	branler	36	catapulter	36
beurrer	36	braquer	36	causer	36
biaiser	36	braver	36	céder	41
bichonner	36	bredouiller	36	ceindre	71
biffer	36	breveter	30	célébrer	41
blaguer	36	bricoler	36	celer	1
blâmer	36	brider	36	censurer	36
blanchir	45	briguer	36	cercler	36
blaser	36	briller	36	certifier	25
blêmir	45	brimer	36	cesser	36
blesser	36	briser	36	chagriner	36
bloquer	36	broder	36	chahuter	36
blottir (se)	45	broncher	36	chamailler	36
boire	12	brosser	36	chanceler	4
boiter	36	brouiller	36	changer	54
bombarder	36	broyer	63	chanter	36
bondir	45	brûler	36	chantonner	36
bonifier	25	brunir	45	charger	54
border	36	buter	36	charmer	36
borner	36	cabrer (se)	36	charrier	25
boucher	36	cacher	36	chasser	36
boucler	36	cadrer	36	châtier	25
bouder	36	cajoler	36	chatouiller	36
bouffer	36	calculer	36	chauffer	36
bouffir	45	caler	36	chausser	36
bouger	54	câliner	36	chercher	36
bouillir	13	calmer	36	chérir	45
bouleverser	36	calomnier	25	chiffrer	36
boulonner	36	calquer	36	choir	*page 13*
bourdonner	36	camper	36	choisir	45
bourrer	36	capituler	36	chômer	36
boursoufler	36	capter	36	choquer	36
bousculer	36	captiver	36	choyer	63

chuchoter	36	complimenter	36	constater	36
circoncire[8]	97	compliquer	36	consterner	36
circonscrire	38	comporter	36	constituer	36
circonvenir[1]	108	composer	36	construire	29
circuler	36	composter	36	consulter	36
cirer	36	**comprendre**	**16**	contacter	36
ciseler	1	compromettre	79	contaminer	36
citer	36	compter	36	contempler	36
clarifier	25	concéder	41	contenir	101
classer	36	concentrer	36	contenter	36
classifier	25	concerner	36	conter	36
cligner	36	concevoir	81	contester	36
clignoter	36	concilier	25	continuer	36
clore	**14**	**conclure**	**17**	contraindre	23
clouer	36	concourir	21	contrarier	25
coder	36	concurrencer	15	contraster	36
codifier	25	condamner	36	contredire	48
cogner	36	condenser	36	contrefaire	43
coiffer	36	condescendre[1]	31	contrevenir[1]	108
coincer	15	**conduire**	**18**	contribuer	36
coïncider	36	conférer	41	contrôler	36
collaborer	36	confier	36	convaincre	105
collectionner	36	confire[9]	97	convenir[1]	108
coller	36	confirmer	36	convertir	45
coloniser	36	confisquer	36	convier	25
colorer	36	confondre	84	convoquer	36
colorier	25	conforter	36	coopérer	41
combattre	11	congédier	25	copier	25
combler	36	congeler	1	correspondre	84
commander	36	**connaître**	**19**	corriger	54
commémorer	36	conquérir	2	corrompre	90
commencer	**15**	consacrer	36	corroyer	63
commettre	56	conseiller	36	côtoyer	63
communier	25	consentir	92	coucher	36
communiquer	36	considérer	41	**coudre**	**20**
comparaître	67	consister	36	couler	36
comparer	36	consoler	36	couper	36
compenser	36	consolider	36	courber	36
complaire	74	consommer	36	**courir**	**21**
compléter	41	conspirer	36	coûter	36

couvrir	22	déboutonner	36	décourager	54
cracher	36	débrailler (se)	36	**découvrir**	**30**
craindre	23	débrancher	36	décréter	41
craquer	36	débrayer	70	décrier	25
créer	24	débrouiller	36	décrire	38
crépir	45	débuter	36	décrocher	36
creuser	36	décaler	36	décroître[10]	27
crever	52	décanter	36	dédaigner	36
cribler	36	décaper	36	dédicacer	15
crier	25	décapoter	36	dédier	25
critiquer	36	décéder[2]	41	dédire	48
crocheter	1	déceler	1	dédommager	54
croire	26	décélérer	41	dédouaner	36
croiser	36	décentraliser	36	dédoubler	36
croître	27	décerner	36	déduire	29
crouler	36	décevoir	81	défaillir[11]	7
croupir	36	déchaîner	36	défaire	43
crucifier	25	décharger	54	défalquer	36
cueillir	28	déchiffrer	36	défavoriser	36
cuire	29	déchiqueter	50	défendre	107
culbuter	36	déchirer	36	déférer	41
cultiver	36	déchoir	*page 13*	déficeler	4
cumuler	36	décider	36	défier	25
curer	36	décimer	36	défigurer	36
daigner	36	déclamer	36	défiler	36
damner	36	déclarer	36	définir	45
danser	36	déclasser	36	défoncer	15
dater	36	déclencher	36	déformer	36
débarquer	36	décliner	36	défraîchir	45
débarrasser	36	décoder	36	dégager	54
débattre	11	décolérer	41	dégainer	36
débaucher	36	décoller	36	dégauchir	45
débiliter	36	décommander	36	dégazonner	36
débiter	36	déconcerter	36	dégeler	1
déblatérer	41	déconseiller	36	dégénérer	41
débloquer	36	décontracter	36	dégonfler	36
déboîter	36	décorer	36	dégourdir	45
déborder	36	découdre	20	dégoûter	36
déboucher	36	découler	36	dégrader	36
débourser	36	découper	36	dégringoler	36

243

dégriser	36	départager	54	désennuyer	63
déguerpir	45	départir (se)	68	désensibiliser	36
déguiser	36	dépasser	69	désentraver	36
déguster	36	dépayser	36	déséquilibrer	36
déjeter	50	dépecer	52	déserter	36
déjeuner	36	dépêcher	36	désespérer	41
déjouer	36	dépeindre	71	déshabiller	36
délaisser	36	dépendre	107	déshabituer	36
délayer	70	dépenser	36	déshériter	36
déléguer	41	dépérir	45	désigner	36
délibérer	41	dépister	36	désinfecter	36
délier	25	déplacer	15	désintégrer	41
délirer	36	déplaire	74	désintéresser	36
délivrer	36	déplier	25	désintoxiquer	36
déloger	54	déployer	63	désirer	36
demander	36	dépolir	45	désister (se)	36
démanteler	1	déposer	36	désobéir	45
démarquer	36	dépouiller	36	désoler	36
démarrer	36	dépoussiérer	41	désorganiser	36
démêler	36	déprécier	25	désorienter	36
déménager	54	déprendre	78	dessaisir	45
démener (se)	52	déprimer	36	dessécher	41
démentir	92	déraciner	36	desserrer	36
démettre	56	déranger	54	dessiner	36
demeurer[12]	36	déraper	36	destiner	36
démissionner	36	dérégler	41	destituer	36
démolir	45	déroger	54	désunir	45
démonter[1]	57	dérouler	36	détacher	36
démontrer	36	dérouter	36	détailler	36
démultiplier	25	désaccoutumer	36	détecter	36
démunir	45	désagréger	80	déteindre	71
dénaturer	36	désaltérer	41	dételer	4
dénier	25	désamorcer	15	détendre	107
dénigrer	36	désapprendre	5	détenir	101
déniveler	4	désapprouver	36	détériorer	36
dénombrer	36	désassortir	45	déterminer	36
dénoncer	15	désavantager	54	détester	36
dénouer	36	désavouer	36	détordre	58
dépanner	36	**descendre**⋆	31	détourner	36
dépaqueter	50	désemparer	36	détraquer	36

détromper	36	distribuer	36
détruire	**32**	diversifier	25
dévaler	36	diviser	36
devancer	15	divorcer	15
développer	36	**donner**	**36**
devenir	**33**	**dormir**	**37**
déverser	36	doubler	36
dévêtir	109	douter	36
dévier	25	dresser	36
deviner	36	durcir	45
dévisser	36	durer	36
dévoiler	36	ébahir (s')	45
devoir	**34**	ébattre (s')	11
dévorer	36	ébaucher	36
dévouer	36	éblouir	45
dicter	36	ébranler	36
différer	41	écarteler	1
diffuser	36	écarter	36
digérer	41	échanger	54
diluer	36	échapper	36
diminuer	36	échauder	36
dîner	36	échauffer	36
dire	**35**	échelonner	36
diriger	54	échoir *page 13*	
disconvenir	108	échouer	36
discourir	21	éclabousser	36
discriminer	36	éclaircir	45
discuter	36	éclairer	36
disjoindre	51	éclater	36
disparaître	67	éclipser	36
dispenser	36	éclore[14]	14
disperser	36	écœurer	36
disposer	36	éconduire	18
disputer	36	économiser	36
dissocier	25	écorcher	36
dissoudre[13]	85	écouler	36
distendre	107	écouter	36
distinguer	36	écraser	36
distordre	58	écrémer	41
distraire	104	écrier (s')	25

écrire	**38**
écrouler (s')	36
édifier	25
éditer	36
éduquer	36
effacer	15
effarer	36
effaroucher	36
effectuer	36
effeuiller	36
effondrer	36
efforcer (s')	15
effrayer	70
égaler	36
égarer	36
égayer	70
égorger	54
élaborer	36
élancer (s')	15
élargir	45
électrifier	25
élever	52
éliminer	36
élire	53
éloigner	36
élouer	36
émanciper	36
émaner	36
embarrasser	36
embaucher	36
embellir	45
emboîter	36
embourgeoiser (s')	
	36
embrasser	36
émerger	54
émettre	56
émigrer	36
emménager	54
emmener	52

émouvoir[15]	61	enjoliver	36	épater	36
emparer (s')	36	enlacer	15	épeler	4
empêcher	36	enlever	52	éplucher	36
empiéter	41	enneiger	54	éponger	94
empirer	36	ennuyer	63	épouser	36
emplir	45	énoncer	15	épouvanter	36
employer	63	enquérir (s')	2	épreindre	71
empoisonner	36	enquêter	36	éprendre (s')	78
emporter	36	enraciner	36	éprouver	36
emprisonner	36	enrager	54	épuiser	36
emprunter	36	enregistrer	36	équilibrer	36
encadrer	36	enrichir	45	équiper	36
encaisser	36	enrouler	36	équivaloir	106
enchaîner	36	enseigner	36	esclaffer (s')	36
enchanter	36	ensevelir	45	escorter	36
encombrer	36	ensuivre (s')[3]	98	espérer	41
encourager	54	entamer	36	esquisser	36
encourir	21	entasser	36	esquiver	36
endetter	36	entendre	107	essayer	70
endoctriner	36	enterrer	36	essorer	36
endommager	54	enthousiasmer	36	essouffler	36
endormir (s')	37	entourer	36	essuyer	63
enduire	29	entraîner	36	estimer	36
endurcir	45	entraver	36	estropier	25
énerver	36	entrelacer	15	établir	45
enfanter	36	entremettre (s')	56	étaler	36
enfermer	36	entreprendre	78	étayer	70
enfiler	36	entrer*	39	éteindre	71
enflammer	36	entretenir	101	étendre	107
enfler	36	entrevoir	111	éternuer	36
enfoncer	15	énumérer	41	étiqueter	50
enfouir	45	envahir	45	étirer	36
enfreindre	71	envelopper	36	étoffer	36
enfuir (s')	46	envisager	54	étonner	36
engager	54	envoler (s')	36	étouffer	36
engloutir	45	envoyer	40	étourdir	45
engourdir	45	épandre	107	étrangler	36
engraisser	36	épanouir	45	être	42
engueuler	36	épargner	36	étreindre	71
enivrer	36	éparpiller	36	étudier	25

246

évader (s')	36	exterminer	36	flairer	36
évaluer	36	extraire	104	flamber	36
évanouir (s')	45	exulter	36	flâner	36
évaporer	36	fabriquer	36	flanquer	36
éveiller	36	fâcher	36	flatter	36
éventer	36	faciliter	36	fléchir	45
évertuer (s')	36	façonner	36	flétrir	45
éviter	36	facturer	36	fleurir[16]	45
évoluer	36	faillir	page 13	flotter	36
évoquer	36	**faire**	**43**	foisonner	36
exagérer	41	**falloir**	**44**	fomenter	36
exalter	36	falsifier	25	foncer	15
examiner	36	familiariser	36	fonctionner	36
exaspérer	41	farcir	45	fonder	36
excéder	41	fasciner	36	fondre	84
excepter	36	fatiguer	36	forcer	15
exciter	36	faucher	36	forger	54
exclamer (s')	36	faufiler	36	formaliser (se)	36
exclure	17	fausser	36	former	36
excommunier	25	favoriser	36	formuler	36
excuser	36	feindre	71	fortifier	25
exécrer	41	feinter	36	foudroyer	63
exécuter	36	fêler	36	fouetter	36
exempter	36	féliciter	36	fouiller	36
exhiber	36	fendre	107	fourmiller	36
exhorter	36	ferler	36	fournir	45
exiger	54	fermenter	36	fourrer	36
exiler	36	fermer	36	fourvoyer	63
exister	36	fêter	36	fracasser	36
exonérer	41	feuilleter	50	franchir	45
expédier	25	fiancer	15	frapper	36
expérimenter	36	ficeler	4	frayer	70
expirer	36	ficher	36	freiner	36
expliquer	36	fier	25	frémir	45
exploiter	36	figer	54	fréquenter	36
exploser	36	filer	36	frire[17]	97
exporter	36	fileter	1	friser	36
exposer	36	financer	15	frissonner	36
exprimer	36	**finir**	**45**	froisser	36
expulser	36	fixer	36	frôler	36

froncer	15	gravir	45	heurter	36
frotter	36	greffer	36	hocher	36
frustrer	36	grêler	36	honorer	36
fuir	**46**	griffonner	36	horrifier	25
fumer	36	grignoter	36	huer	36
fusiller	36	griller	36	humaniser	36
gâcher	36	grimacer	15	humidifier	25
gagner	36	grimper	36	humilier	25
galoper	36	grincer	15	hurler	36
garantir	45	griser	36	hypnotiser	36
garder	36	grogner	36	idéaliser	36
garer	36	grommeler	4	identifier	25
garnir	45	gronder	36	ignorer	36
gaspiller	36	grossir	45	illuminer	36
gâter	36	grouiller	36	illustrer	36
gauchir	45	grouper	36	imaginer	36
gaufrer	36	guérir	45	imiter	36
gausser (se)	36	guerroyer	63	immigrer	36
geindre	71	guetter	36	immiscer (s')	15
geler	1	guider	36	immobiliser	36
gémir	45	guinder	36	immoler	36
gêner	36	habiller	36	impatienter	36
généraliser	36	habiter	36	impliquer	36
gérer	41	habituer	36	implorer	36
gésir	page 13	hacher	36	importer	36
giboyer	63	**haïr**	**47**	impressionner	36
gifler	36	haleter	1	imprimer	36
givrer	36	handicaper	36	improviser	36
glacer	15	hanter	36	inaugurer	36
glisser	36	harceler	4	inciter	36
glorifier	25	harmoniser	36	incliner	36
gommer	36	hasarder	36	inclure[18]	17
gonfler	36	hâter	36	incommoder	36
goûter	36	hausser	36	incorporer	36
gouverner	36	héberger	54	incriminer	36
gracier	25	hébéter	41	inculper	36
grandir	45	hennir	45	indiquer	36
gratifier	25	hérisser	36	induire	29
gratter	36	hériter	36	infecter	36
graver	36	hésiter	36	infester	36

infirmer	36	invoquer	36	lorgner	36
infliger	54	irriter	36	lotir	45
influencer	15	isoler	36	loucher	36
informer	36	jaillir	45	louer	36
ingénier (s')	25	jaser	36	louper	36
inhaler	36	jaunir	45	louvoyer	63
initier	25	**jeter**	**50**	lubrifier	25
injurier	25	jeûner	36	lutter	36
innover	36	**joindre**	**51**	mâcher	36
inoculer	36	jouer	36	machiner	36
inonder	36	jouir	45	magnifier	25
inquiéter	41	juger	54	maigrir	45
inscrire	38	jumeler	4	maintenir	101
insensibiliser	36	jurer	36	maîtriser	36
insérer	41	justifier	25	majorer	36
insinuer	36	labourer	36	malfaire	43
insister	36	lacer	15	malmener	52
inspecter	36	lâcher	36	maltraiter	36
inspirer	36	laisser	36	**manger**	**54**
installer	36	lamenter (se)	36	manier	25
instituer	36	lancer	15	manifester	36
instruire	29	languir	45	manigancer	15
insulter	36	larmoyer	63	manipuler	36
insurger (s')	54	laver	36	manœuvrer	36
intégrer	41	lécher	41	manquer	36
intensifier	25	légaliser	36	manufacturer	36
intercéder	41	légiférer	41	manutentionner	36
interdire	**48**	lésiner	36	marcher	36
intéresser	36	**lever**	**52**	marier	25
interloquer	36	libérer	41	marquer	36
interroger	54	licencier	25	marteler	1
interrompre	90	lier	25	masquer	36
intervenir	108	ligoter	36	massacrer	36
intituler	36	limer	36	masser	36
intriguer	36	limiter	36	matérialiser	36
introduire	**49**	liquéfier	25	**maudire**	**55**
inventer	36	liquider	36	maugréer	24
invertir	45	**lire**	**53**	mécaniser	36
investir	45	livrer	36	méconnaître	19
inviter	36	loger	54	mécontenter	36

médire	48	mortifier	25	obliger	54
méditer	36	motiver	36	oblitérer	41
méfaire	43	moucher	36	obscurcir	45
méfier (se)	25	**moudre**	**59**	obséder	41
mélanger	54	mouiller	36	observer	36
mêler	36	**mourir**	**60**	obstiner (s')	36
menacer	15	**mouvoir**	**61**	obtenir	**64**
ménager	54	muer	36	occuper	36
mendier	25	multiplier	25	octroyer	63
mener	52	munir	45	offenser	36
mentionner	36	mûrir	45	**offrir**	**65**
mentir	92	murmurer	36	oindre	page 13
méprendre (se)	78	museler	4	omettre	56
mépriser	36	muter	36	opérer	41
mériter	36	mutiler	36	opposer	36
messeoir	page 13	mystifier	25	opprimer	36
mesurer	36	nager	54	ordonner	36
mettre	**56**	**naître**	**62**	organiser	36
meubler	36	nantir	45	orner	36
meugler	36	narrer	36	orthographier	25
meurtrir	45	naviguer	36	osciller	36
miauler	36	navrer	36	oser	36
mijoter	36	nécessiter	36	ôter	36
mimer	36	négliger	54	oublier	25
miner	36	négocier	25	ouïr	page 13
minimiser	36	neiger	54	outrager	54
mobiliser	36	**nettoyer**	**63**	**ouvrir**	**66**
modeler	1	nier	25	oxyder	36
modérer	41	niveler	4	pacifier	25
moderniser	36	noircir	45	paître	page 13
modifier	25	nommer	36	pâlir	45
moisir	45	normaliser	36	palper	36
moissonner	36	noter	36	palpiter	36
mollir	45	nouer	36	panser	36
monnayer	70	nourrir	45	parachever	52
monopoliser	36	noyer	63	parachuter	36
monter*	**57**	nuire[19]	29	**paraître**	**67**
montrer	36	numéroter	36	paralyser	36
moquer (se)	36	obéir	45	parcourir	21
mordre	**58**	objecter	36	pardonner	36

parer	36	pétrifier	25	prédire	48		
parfondre	84	pétrir	45	préférer	41		
parfumer	36	peupler	36	préjuger	54		
parier	25	photographier	36	prélever	52		
parler	36	picoter	36	préméditer	36		
parquer	36	piéger	80	**prendre**	**78**		
partager	54	piétiner	36	préparer	36		
participer	36	pincer	15	prescrire	38		
partir	**68**	placer	15	présenter	36		
parvenir	108	plaider	36	préserver	36		
passer★	**69**	plaindre	23	présider	36		
passionner	36	**plaire**	**74**	pressentir	92		
patienter	36	plaisanter	36	présumer	36		
pâtir	45	planifier	25	prétendre	107		
pauser	36	plaquer	36	prêter	36		
paver	36	pleurer	36	prévaloir[21]	106		
pavoiser	36	**pleuvoir**	**75**	prévenir[1]	108		
payer	**70**	plier	25	prévoir[22]	111		
pêcher	36	plonger	94	prier	25		
pécher	41	poindre	*page 13*	priver	36		
peigner	36	polir	45	privilégier	25		
peindre	**71**	polluer	36	procéder	41		
peler	1	pomper	36	proclamer	36		
pencher	36	ponctuer	36	procréer	24		
pendre	107	pondre	84	produire	29		
pénétrer	41	porter	36	profiter	36		
penser	36	poser	36	progresser	36		
percer	15	posséder	41	projeter	50		
percevoir	81	poster	36	prolonger	94		
perdre	**72**	poudroyer	63	promener	52		
perfectionner	36	pourfendre	107	**promettre**	**79**		
perforer	36	pourrir	45	promouvoir[23]	61		
périr	45	poursuivre	98	prononcer	15		
permettre	**73**	pousser	36	proposer	36		
persécuter	36	**pouvoir**[20]	**77**	proscrire	38		
persévérer	41	pratiquer	36	**protéger**	**80**		
persister	36	précéder	41	protester	36		
persuader	36	prêcher	36	prouver	36		
pervertir	45	préciser	36	provenir	108		
peser	52			publier	25		

punir	45	rassembler	36	recueillir	28
purifier	25	rasséréner	41	recuire	29
qualifier	25	rassurer	36	reculer	36
quereller	36	rater	36	récupérer	41
questionner	36	rationaliser	36	recycler	36
quêter	36	rattraper	36	redescendre	31
quitter	36	ravir	45	rédiger	54
rabattre	11	ravitailler	36	redire	35
raccommoder	36	réagir	45	redoubler	36
raccompagner	36	réaliser	36	redouter	36
raccorder	36	rebattre	11	redresser	36
raccourcir	45	rebondir	45	réduire	29
raccrocher	36	rebuter	36	refaire	43
racheter	1	recenser	36	référer	41
racler	36	receler	1	refermer	36
racoler	**36**	réchapper	36	réfléchir	45
raconter	36	réchauffer	36	refléter	41
raffermir	45	rechercher	36	refondre	84
raffiner	36	réciter	36	réformer	36
rafler	36	réclamer	36	refroidir	45
rafraîchir	45	récolter	36	réfugier (se)	25
ragaillardir	45	recommander	36	refuser	36
raidir	45	recommencer	15	réfuter	36
railler	36	récompenser	36	regagner	36
raisonner	36	réconcilier	25	regaillardir	45
rajeunir	45	reconduire	18	regarder	36
rajouter	36	réconforter	36	régénérer	41
rajuster	36	reconnaître	19	régir	45
ralentir	45	reconquérir	2	régler	41
rallier	25	reconstruire	29	régner	41
rallonger	94	reconvertir	45	regretter	36
rallumer	36	recopier	25	regrouper	36
ramasser	36	recoudre	20	réhabiliter	36
ramener	52	recourir	21	réhabituer	36
ramollir	45	recouvrir	22	rehausser	36
ranimer	36	récréer	36	réimprimer	36
rappeler	4	récrier (se)	25	réintégrer	41
rapporter	36	récrire	38	rejaillir	45
rapprocher	36	rectifier	25	rejeter	50
raser	36			rejoindre	51

réjouir	45	renouveler	4	restreindre	71
relâcher	36	rénover	36	résulter	36
relancer	15	renseigner	36	résumer	36
reléguer	41	**rentrer***	**83**	resurgir	45
relever	52	renverser	36	rétablir	45
relier	25	renvoyer	40	retaper	36
relire	53	réorganiser	36	retarder	36
reluire[24]	29	repaître	*page 13*	retenir	101
remanier	25	répandre	107	retirer	36
remarier	25	reparaître	67	retomber	102
remarquer	36	réparer	36	**retourner***	**87**
rembourser	36	repartir	68	retrancher	36
remédier	25	répartir	45	retransmettre	56
remercier	25	repeindre	71	rétrécir	45
remettre	56	rependre	107	retrousser	36
remmener	52	repentir (se)	92	retrouver	36
remonter	57	reperdre	72	réunir	45
remontrer	36	répéter	41	réussir	45
remordre	58	**répondre**	**84**	revaloir	106
remorquer	36	repousser	36	réveiller	36
remoudre	59	reprendre	78	révéler	41
remplacer	15	représenter	36	revendiquer	36
remplir	45	reproduire	29	revendre	107
employer	63	répudier	25	**revenir**	**88**
remporter	36	requérir	2	rêver	36
remuer	36	réserver	36	révérer	41
renaître[25]	62	résider	36	revêtir	109
renchérir	45	résigner	36	réviser	36
rencontrer	36	résilier	25	revivre	110
rendormir	37	résister	36	revoir	111
rendre	**82**	résonner	36	révolter	36
renduire	29	**résoudre**	**85**	rhabiller	36
renfermer	36	respirer	36	ridiculiser	36
renfler	36	resplendir	45	rigoler	36
renforcer	15	ressaisir	45	**rire**	**89**
renier	25	ressembler	36	risquer	36
renifler	36	ressemeler	4	rivaliser	36
renommer	36	ressentir	92	rogner	36
renoncer	15	ressortir	95	**rompre**	**90**
renouer	36	**rester**	**86**	ronfler	36

253

ronger	94	simplifier	25	**suivre**	**98**
rôtir	45	simuler	36	supplier	25
rougir	45	soigner	36	supposer	36
rouler	36	sombrer	36	surcharger	54
rouspéter	41	sommeiller	36	surenchérir	45
rouvrir	66	**songer**	**94**	surfaire	43
ruiner	36	sonner	36	surgeler	1
saccager	54	**sortir***	**95**	surgir	45
saisir	45	souffrir	65	surmonter[1]	57
salir	45	souhaiter	36	surpasser	69
saluer	36	souiller	36	surprendre	78
sanctifier	25	soulager	54	**surseoir**	**99**
sangloter	36	soulever	52	surveiller	36
satisfaire	43	souligner	36	survenir	108
sauter	36	soumettre	56	survivre	110
sauvegarder	36	soupçonner	36	susciter	36
sauver	36	soupeser	52	suspendre	107
savoir	**91**	sourire	89	tacher	36
scier	25	souscrire	38	tâcher	36
scinder	36	sous-entendre	107	tailler	36
scintiller	36	soustraire	104	**taire (se)**	**100**
sécher	41	soutenir	101	taper	36
secouer	36	**souvenir (se)**	**96**	tâter	36
secourir	21	spécialiser	36	taxer	36
séduire	29	spécifier	25	teindre	71
sembler	36	standardiser	36	teinter	36
semer	52	stationner	36	téléphoner	36
sentir	**92**	stériliser	36	téléviser	36
seoir	page 13	stimuler	36	témoigner	36
séparer	36	stupéfier	25	tendre	107
serrer	36	subir	45	**tenir**	**101**
sertir	45	submerger	54	tenter	36
servir	**93**	subsister	36	terminer	36
sévir	45	substituer	36	ternir	45
sevrer	52	substituer	108	terrasser	36
siéger	80	succéder	41	terrifier	25
siffler	36	sucer	15	téter	41
signaler	36	suer	36	tiédir	45
signer	36	**suffire**	**97**	timbrer	36
signifier	25	suggérer	41	tirer	36

tolérer	41	tricher	36	verdoyer	63
tomber	**102**	tricoter	36	vérifier	25
tondre	84	trier	25	vernir	45
tonner	36	triompher	36	verrouiller	36
tordre	58	tripoter	36	verser	36
torpiller	36	tromper	36	**vêtir**	**109**
tortiller	36	troquer	36	vexer	36
torturer	36	trotter	36	vibrer	36
toucher	36	troubler	36	vider	36
tourmenter	36	trouer	36	vieillir	45
tourner	36	trouver	36	violer	36
tournoyer	63	truffer	36	virer	36
tousser	36	truquer	36	viser	36
tracasser	36	tuer	36	visiter	36
tracer	15	tutoyer	63	visser	36
traduire	**103**	ulcérer	41	vitrifier	25
trahir	45	unifier	25	vitupérer	41
traîner	36	unir	45	vivifier	25
traire	**104**	urbaniser	36	**vivre**	**110**
traiter	36	user	36	vociférer	41
transcrire	38	usiner	36	voiler	36
transférer	41	utiliser	36	**voir**	**111**
transformer	36	vacciner	36	voler	36
transmettre	56	**vaincre**	**105**	vomir	45
transparaître	67	**valoir**	**106**	voter	36
transpirer	36	vanter	36	vouer	36
transplanter	36	varier	25	**vouloir**	**112**
transporter	36	végéter	41	vouvoyer	63
traquer	36	veiller	36	voyager	54
travailler	36	vendanger	54	vrombir	45
traverser	36	**vendre**	**107**	vulgariser	36
trébucher	36	venger	36	zébrer	41
trembler	36	**venir**	**108**	zézayer	70
tremper	36	verdir	45	zigzaguer	36

NOTES

1) *Auxiliary* = avoir.
2) *Auxiliary* = être.
3) *Only infinitive and 3rd persons of each tense used.*
4) *Past participle:* absous, absoute; *Past Historic and Past Subjunctive not used.*
5) *Conjugated with either* avoir *or* être.
6) *No circumflex on:* j'accrois, tu accrois, j'accrus, tu accrus, il accrut, ils accrurent, j'accrusse *etc,* accru.
7) *Hardly used except in infinitive and 3rd persons of Present, Future and Conditional.*
8) *Past participle:* circoncis.
9) *Past participle:* confit.
10) *As for (6).*
11) *Present tense singular, Future and Conditional tenses least common.*
12) *'To live': auxiliary* = avoir; *'to remain': auxiliary* = être.
13) *Past participle:* dissous, dissoute; *Past Historic and Past Subjunctive not used.*
14) *Auxiliary* = être; *NB:* il éclot; *hardly used except in 3rd persons.*
15) *Past participle:* ému.
16) *'To prosper': present participle* = florissant; *Imperfect* = florissait.
17) *Past participle:* frit; *used mainly in singular of Present tense and in compound tenses.*
18) *Past participle:* inclus.
19) *Past participle:* nui.
20) *In interrogative form, 'puis' is substituted for 'peux':* puis-je vous aider? = *may I help you?*
21) *Present Subjunctive:* je prévale *etc.*
22) *Future:* je prévoirai *etc; Conditional:* je prévoirais *etc.*
23) *Past participle:* promu; *used only in infinitive, both participles, and compound tenses.*
24) *Past participle:* relui; *Past Historic:* je reluis *etc.*
25) *No past participle – no compound tenses.*